Lawyer Marketing Series™

Google+ For Lawyers

A Step by Step User's Guide

By MICHAEL WADDINGTON, ESQ
&
ALEXANDRA GONZALEZ-WADDINGTON, ESQ

Google+ For Lawyers: A Step by Step User's Guide

Published by
Legal Niche Pros, LLC
601 North Belair Square, Suite 16
Evans, GA 30809
www.legalnichepros.com

Printed in the United States of America

First Printing: September 2013

ISBN-13: 978-0615853727 (Lawyer Marketing Series)

ISBN-10: 0615853722

Table of Contents

ABOUT THE AUTHORS

Michael Waddington, Esq. - Michael started building and marketing websites in 1997 while still a 1L at Temple University School of Law. Now a nationally-recognized expert on Internet marketing for lawyers, he is the founder of *Legal Niche Pros, LLC,* a boutique Internet marketing firm that specializes in video marketing, website design, social media, and search engine marketing.

As creator of the *Lawyer Marketing Series*™, a series of educational books and instructional marketing videos for attorneys, Michael is a noted commentator, writer, and lecturer on Internet marketing and lawyer marketing ethics. His *Lawyer Marketing* YouTube channel currently has over 2,500 subscribers, and his video tutorial series "60 Second SEO Tips" is widely viewed on YouTube and LinkedIn. In 2013, Michael contributed a chapter on Internet marketing to Jack Canfield's best-selling book, *Dare to Succeed.* (Canfield is the best-selling author of *Chicken Soup for the Soul.*)

Licensed to practice law in Pennsylvania, Georgia, New Jersey, and South Carolina, Michael's high-profile criminal cases have made the cover of the *New York Times*, *Rolling Stone* magazine, *The New Yorker*, *People*, and other national publications. He has been quoted by hundreds of major media outlets worldwide and provided consultation services to CBS news, *60 Minutes*, *ABC News Nightline*, the BBC, CNN, CBS, German Public Television, as well as the Golden Globe-winning TV series, *The Good Wife.*

Appearing in the 2009 CNN 1-hour documentary "Killings at the Canal," Waddington's cases have been the subject of numerous movies and books including the Academy Award-winning film *Taxi to the Dark Side,* the 2013 documentary *The Kill Team*, the 2007 Brian De Palma war film *Redacted*, and the popular books *Strike and Destroy* and *The Good Soldier on Trial*. Michael also co-authored the American Bar Association book, "The State of Criminal Justice 2013."

For more information visit: www.legalnichepros.com.

Alexandra Gonzalez-Waddington, Esq. – Alexandra is a practicing lawyer, licensed mediator, and founding partner of *Legal Niche Pros, LLC*. With over a decade of experience in Internet marketing, she specializes in business consulting for small law firms, brand development, and local marketing. Among her many professional accomplishments, Alexandra has helped dozens of attorneys across the United States build successful law practices and has coached attorneys on effective social media marketing, practice management, business development, and marketing strategy. Alexandra is licensed to practice law--and is a member in good standing--of the State Bar of Georgia.

Chapter 1: Overview

Google+ is the world's second largest social networking site, with over 400 million registered users. Approximately half of the registered users are active users. As direct competition to Facebook, Google+ is linked to all other Google services, such as Gmail (Google's email system), YouTube, and Google Drive (previously Google Docs, their document sharing platform). This gives Google+ an advantage over its competition, which is currently limited to a "one site, one platform" design.

Google+ (pronounced Google Plus, abbreviated as G+ or GPlus) offers features such as Circles, a customizable way to group contacts, and Hangouts, a video chat system capable of linking up to ten contacts at once from your computer, tablet, or phone. Google+ also allows users to import contacts from Yahoo and Hotmail.

Google+ allows photo uploads of full-resolution photos as well as an automatic back-up feature for pictures you take with your phone. These images are stored online in a private album until you determine how you wish to share them. Video uploads are also supported. Like its competitors, Google+ also features customizable communities, where like-minded people can congregate to share ideas and information.

Originally designed as a personal social networking system, Google+, like Facebook, quickly became a platform for business marketing. Welcoming local businesses into the social world, Google launched Google+ Business Pages, a specifically designed network for marketing businesses. Google now mixes their search results with relevant local businesses, pulled from Google+ Business Pages.

Google+ is an indispensable tool for law firms that want to generate business through the Internet. When potential clients search for lawyers, not only will they see the usual search results, they might also see posts, customer reviews, photos, and videos from your law firm's Google+ Business. If you are a lawyer that wants to attract local clients, then you should devote a significant portion of your marketing budget to Google+ Local marketing.

In today's economy, it is wise to take advantage of every available tool to reach potential clients. Law schools are graduating record numbers of new lawyers every year. Many of these new lawyers are entering private practice right out of law school and using the Internet to generate business. A battle to find clients is being waged on the Internet and the competition is fierce. Google+, combined with a comprehensive marketing plan, can give you an edge over other lawyers.

The goal of this book is to show you how to make that happen. This book was written with the intent to help private practice lawyers generate more business through Google+ and the Internet. Please note, when I refer to lawyers or attorneys, I am referring to lawyers engaged in the private practice of law.

Now, more than ever, private practice attorneys must market their services or their business will fail. Lawyers face stiff competition from other law firms as well as from "do it yourself" legal service companies such as LegalZoom.com™.

While some people still use the phone book to find a lawyer, the majority of U.S. consumers rely on the Internet to find and vet a law firm. Lawyers should invest the marketing budget in building a dominant Internet presence rather than spending money on old school advertising such as the phone book.

The purpose of building a dominant Internet presence is to:

    1) Attract not only more, but better clients.

2) Establish yourself as an expert in your field of law.

3) Provide high quality, relevant information to consumers.

4) Expand your professional network and get referrals from other lawyers.

When it comes to Internet marketing, you must be everywhere. Every time someone does a search related to your legal niche and geographic area, you want to be on the first page, more than once if possible. You want your website, videos, social media (Google+), YouTube channel, business listings, and blogs to dominate the local search results.

If you are "everywhere" online, then you are more likely to get calls from potential clients. You also start to establish yourself as an authority in your niche.

With Google+, you can establish yourself as a leader in your niche with other lawyers. Google+ allows you to create a Circle or group related to your niche. For example, you could create a Circle on "Atlanta, GA DUI News" and then invite your colleagues to join the group. In the group, you and your colleagues can post thoughts, ideas, and questions that only they can see.

Another significant feature of Google+ is called Hangout. Hangout is a free but powerful video conferencing tool. A Google+ Hangout allows you to invite up to 10 guests to participate in a live video conference. The video conference can be kept private or can be made public and be posted on your Google+ page and your YouTube channel. This is an excellent way to communicate with colleagues. In addition, Hangouts can be used to record and publish informative videos about your area of legal expertise.

The ability to keep in touch is not limited to your professional network. You can also create a Circle for your clients. You could send out monthly newsletters to your clients for free. You can also do video webinars on timely legal issues and share the videos with your current and future clients. If you are an estate-planning lawyer and Medicare announces new regulations that could impact your clients, you could use Google+ to create an informational video and send it to your clients. In addition, you could also post the video on your website, YouTube channel, and social media sites such as Facebook. You can use these videos as "infomercials" to not only keep clients updated, but to convince them they need to schedule an appointment to update their plans.

In addition, it is worth noting that you can use Google+ to stay connected with family and friends. Google+ has many social networking features similar to Facebook.

Now that you know how Google+ can benefit you and your practice, it is time to learn how to put this tool to work for you.

Chapter 2: Getting Started with Google+

Setting up a Google Account

If you already have a Google account (such as Gmail or Google Drive), use that login information. If not, you need to create a Google account before creating your Google+ page. Your login information (ID and password) will be the same across all Google products.

To set up your Google+ account, open your web browser and go to http://www.plus.google.com. This takes you to the login/sign up page (see Figure 2.1). Once there, click on "Create an account."

GOOGLE+ TIP

When setting up a new Gmail account try to pick an easy-to-remember email address such as your first and last name: michaelwaddington@gmail.com. Or, an email related to your law firm: atlantagatriallawyers@gmail.com or thesmithfirm@gmail.com.

Avoid using numbers, hyphens, periods, or symbols within your Gmail address. This may cause confusion and the address will be more difficult to remember. For example, avoid: Michael.s.waddington@gmail.com, michaelw125465@ gmail.com, michael_waddington$% @ gmail.com.

Also, make sure your Gmail address is professional. Avoid quirky nicknames or words that make you look unprofessional, such as sweet69@gmail.com, poodleluver@gmail .com, or beerpongking1995 @gmail.com.

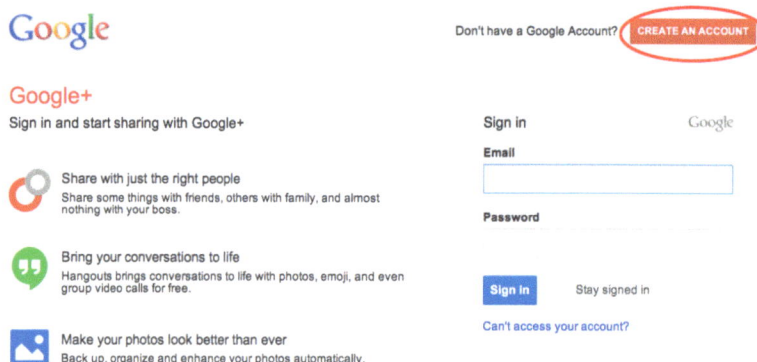

Figure .

Entering Basic Account Information

Google+ requires that you open your account with your personal information, not your practice information. This information remains private. Your clients will not have access to your private information.

If you attempt to open your account with your practice name, your account may be suspended. Once you have created your personal profile, you can create a page for your practice. Next, you must set up your Google+ Profile (see Figure 2.2). Google+ requires basic information to set up your account. You must provide:

- First and last name

- Username (more on that in a moment)

- Password

- Birthday

- Gender

- Mobile phone number

- Email address

When setting up the account, you will be required to prove that you are a human being and not a robot. There are two words in a text box that you are required to retype. Google also asks for your mobile phone number for security reasons.

You must provide Google with accurate cell phone information. If you do not use your actual cell phone, then you may be locked out of your account. If Google detects suspicious activity or detects that someone may be attempting to hack your account, they will verify the security of your account by sending you a text message with a security code. You will then have to enter the code before you can access your account. Make sure you update your Google account if your cell phone number changes.

You can opt out of the text box verification. However, skipping that step may trigger a phone call from Google requesting telephone verification of your identity.

Next, you are required to choose your country of origin in the drop-down box. Below that, you will see two check boxes followed by some text. You must check the first box signifying that you have read and agreed to Google's Terms of Use and Privacy Policy. If this box is not checked, then your account will not be approved. The box below that is automatically checked. This box deals with personalization of +1's, Google's version of Facebook "Likes." Checking this box gives Google permission to use your account information to personalize +1's on non-Google websites.

Create a new Google Account

Your Google Account is more than just Google+.

Talk, chat, share, schedule, store, organize, collaborate, discover, and create. Use Google products from Gmail to Google+ to YouTube, view your search history, all with one username and password, all backed up all the time and easy to find at (you guessed it) Google.com.

Take it all with you.

A Google Account lets you access all your stuff — Gmail, photos, and more — from any device. Search by taking pictures, or by voice. Get free turn-by-turn navigation, upload your pictures automatically, and even buy things with your phone using Google Wallet.

Share a little. Or share a lot.

Share selectively with friends, family (maybe even your boss) on Google+. Start a video call with friends, send a message to a group all at once, or just follow posts from people who fascinate you. Your call.

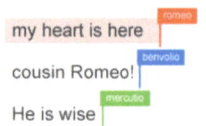

Work in the future.

Get a jump on the next era of doing, well, everything. Watch as colleagues or partners drop in a photo, update a spreadsheet, or improve a paragraph, in real-time, from 1,000 miles away. Google Docs is free with a Google Account.

Name
First   Last

Choose your username
                    @gmail.com

Create a password

Confirm your password

Birthday
Month   ⬍   Day   Year

Gender
I am...   ⬍

Mobile phone
      +17

Your current email address

Prove you're not a robot
      Skip this verification (phone verification may be required)

uartidve posure

Type the two pieces of text:
                              C ◄) ?

Location
United States   ⬍

      I agree to the Google Terms of Service and Privacy Policy

✓   Google may use my account information to personalize +1's on content and ads on non-Google websites. About personalization.

                              Next step

Figure 2.2: Create a new Google Account screen

Adding a Profile Picture

When you have completed the required fields on this screen, click "Next step." The next screen (see Figure 2.3) allows you to utilize the phrase "Putting a Face to Your Name." Given that you are your business, and that you want to be recognized, we suggest uploading a professional looking photo. When you customize your Business Page, you will be able to upload additional images, such as your practice logo or letterhead image.

GOOGLE+ TIP

When uploading photos to Google+, make sure the images are professional and clear. Group photos, a photo of you drinking alcohol, wearing a tank top, or any other photo that does not portray you as a high quality lawyer should not be used. Potential clients will see your images and first impressions make a difference. If you do not have a professional photo, then you should hire a photographer or go to a portrait studio. Your profile photo should generally be a headshot or a head and shoulders shot. If you use unprofessional photos it may cost you clients. You are better off having no photo than having an unprofessional photo.

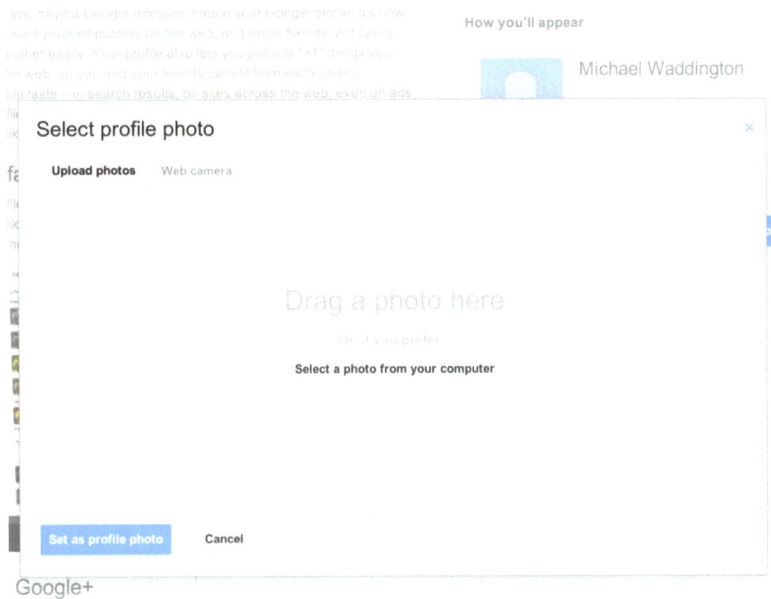

Figure 2.3: Add profile photo

Adding a profile picture is easy. You have two options: Dragging a photo from another folder or your desktop into the area marked "Drag a photo here," or clicking "Select a photo from your computer."

Cropping the Profile Picture

When you have navigated to the folder containing the photo you want to use, double-click the photo to begin the upload. Once the photo uploads, you can move a cropping box to select the area of the photo you want to set as your profile photo. This process will help you correctly size the image (see Figure 2.4).

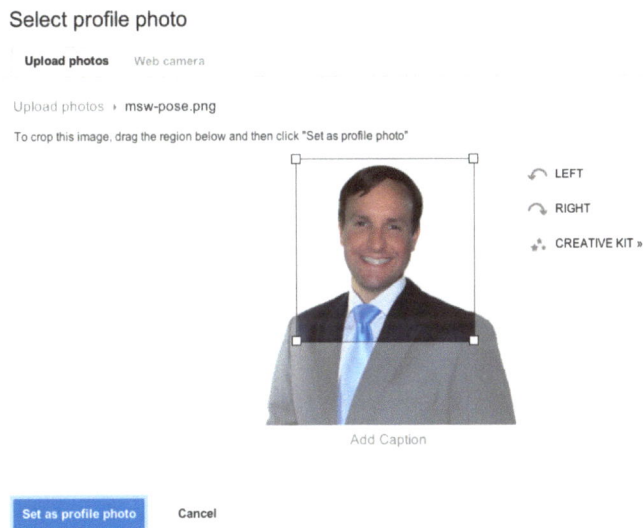

Figure 2.4: Crop the photo

Once you are satisfied with the image, click "Set as profile photo." If you have done everything correctly, you should see the following screen (see Figure 2.5). If you are not satisfied with how it turned out, you can click "Edit photo" and begin the process again. Once you are satisfied, click "Next step."

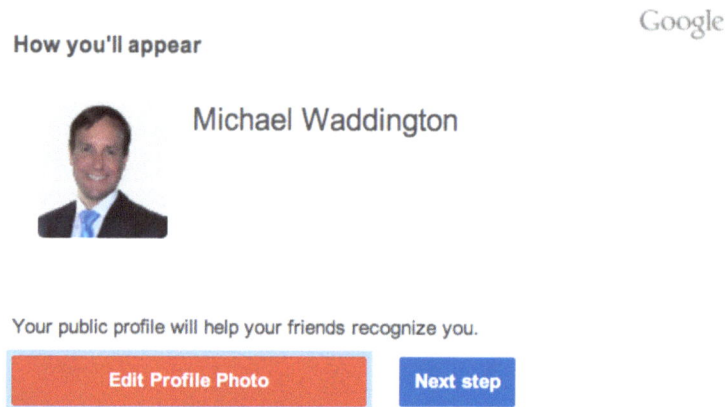

Figure 2.5: Approval screen for profile photo

This takes you to the following screen where you can customize various settings, such as privacy, that affect your profile (see Figure 2.6).

Optimize Profile Settings

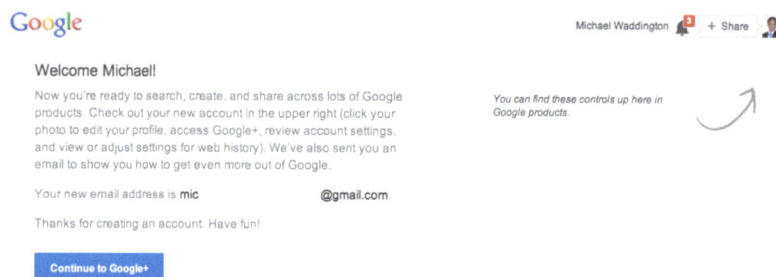

Figure 2.6: Profile complete

Optimizing Profile Settings

Let us take a moment to review Figure 2.6. The welcome dialogue provides several pieces of useful information. You will also find your new email address. This is the username you selected during registration followed by "@gmail.com."

While it may be tempting to jump right in and click the "Continue to Google+" button, we suggest that you take the time to review and modify your profile and account settings. You will notice your full name in the upper right corner of the screen along with a red box containing a number, a dialog box containing "+ Share," and your profile picture with a downward arrow to the right of it.

Dealing with Notifications

The red box indicates that you have notifications from Google and the number tells you how many notifications are waiting for you. Click on it now (see Figure 2.7).

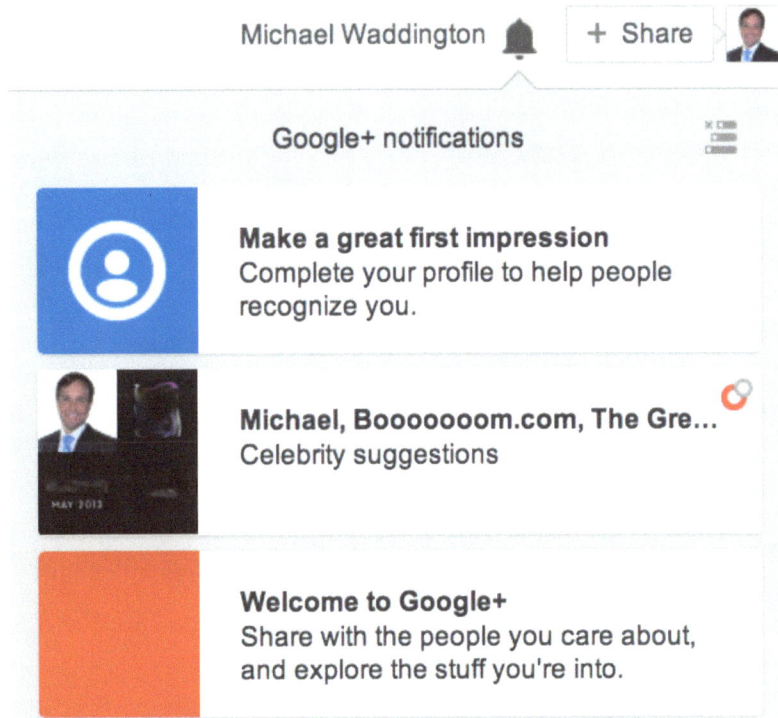

Figure 2.7: Notifications window

As you can see, there's an explanation of notifications. Notifications will appear when someone shares something with you on Google+. When you are finished reading your notifications, simply click anywhere outside the notifications window to close it.

Sharing Content on Google+

Now take a moment to look at "+ Share." This is an important tool to use in reaching your clients. Think of it as posting to Facebook, Twitter, or updating a blog. You can include photos, links to pertinent websites, videos, and even events. This can be a very powerful way of connecting with your clients (see Figure 2.8). When you are finished with the + Share window, simply click anywhere outside of the window to close it. If you actually want to share something, click the "Share" button.

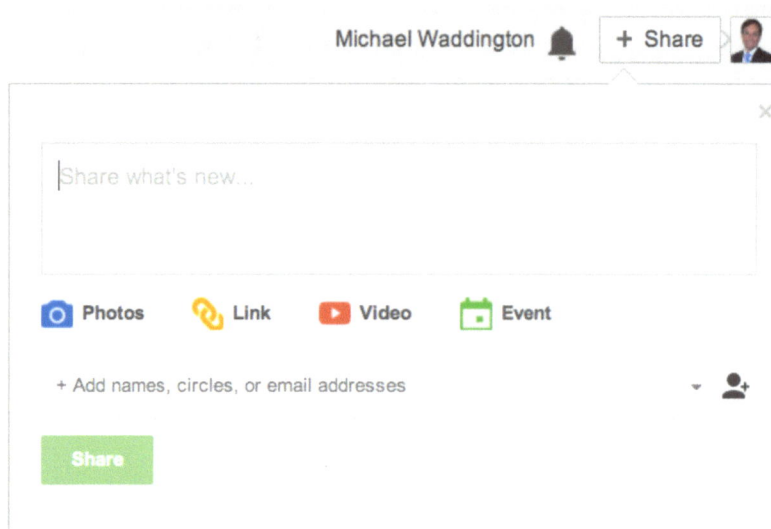

Figure 2.8: + Share window

Before we explore further, let's finish setting up your profile, account, and privacy settings. First, click on your profile picture. This opens a new window showing the following information: Full name, email address, links for Account and Privacy, as well as "View profile" and "Sign out" buttons (see Figure 2.9).

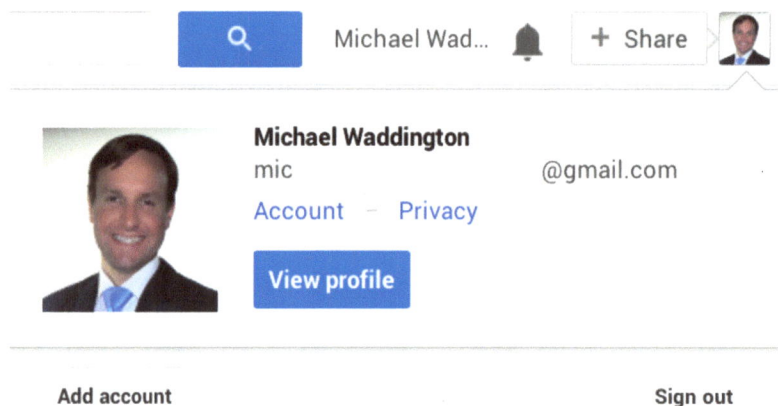

Figure 2.9: View profile window

Setting Up Your Profile

To begin, click on "View profile." This takes you to your profile page (see Figure 2.10). This is where you tell people about yourself and your practice. Remember, this is your personal profile. However, keep the content professional because your clients could potentially view it. You can put as much, or as little, as you wish in your profile. Given that your clients, and potential clients, might be curious as to your background, we suggest that you complete the Work, Story, Education, and Links portions.

GOOGLE+ TIP

You should fill out your profile with as much information as possible regarding your law firm, education, and experience. This will help establish your credibility with potential clients and colleagues. An incomplete profile looks unprofessional. If you have any doubts, go to Google+ and look at lawyer profiles, both personal and professional. Lawyers with robust profiles look more professional than lawyers that are missing basic information such as education, employment, and links to their website and social media sites, such as Avvo, Linkedin, Facebook, etc.

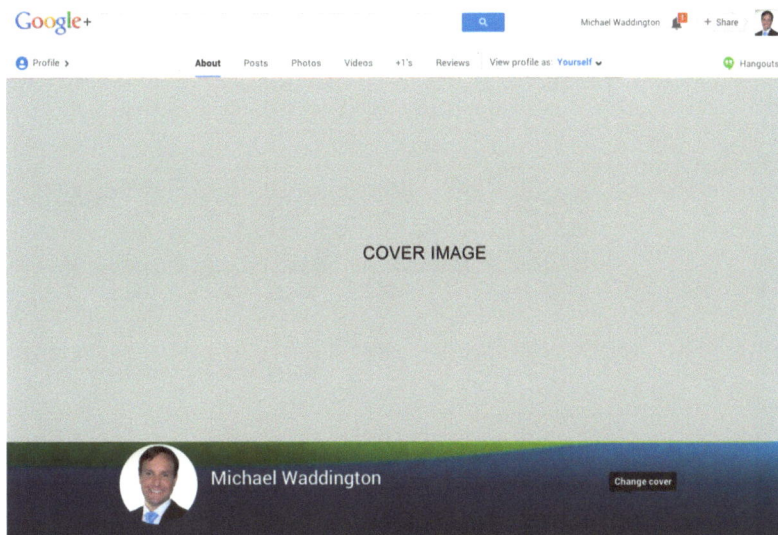

Figure 2.10: Profile page

Selecting a Cover Photo

The first thing you'll notice when viewing your profile is the option to change your cover photo. Your cover photo is not your profile photo. It is the background behind your cover photo. If you elect to change the background, simply click "Change cover" and you'll be shown a selection of backgrounds from which to choose. The process of selecting a new cover photo is exactly the same as selecting your profile photo.

Circles (Contacts)

The first section of your profile we are going to work on is "People." This section shows both the people you have in Circles and the people who have you in their Circles. Since this is a new profile, you have neither at the moment. However, you can import contacts from Yahoo, Hotmail, Gmail, Outlook, Thunderbird, Apple Address Book, and other systems that export information in comma-separated-value (.csv) or vCard (.vcf) format. You can also find coworkers by company name and classmates by school name.

Organizing Contacts

You can organize contacts at this stage into Circles, such as friends, family, client, etc. Begin the import process by clicking on the People link on the left navigation bar (see Figure 2.11).

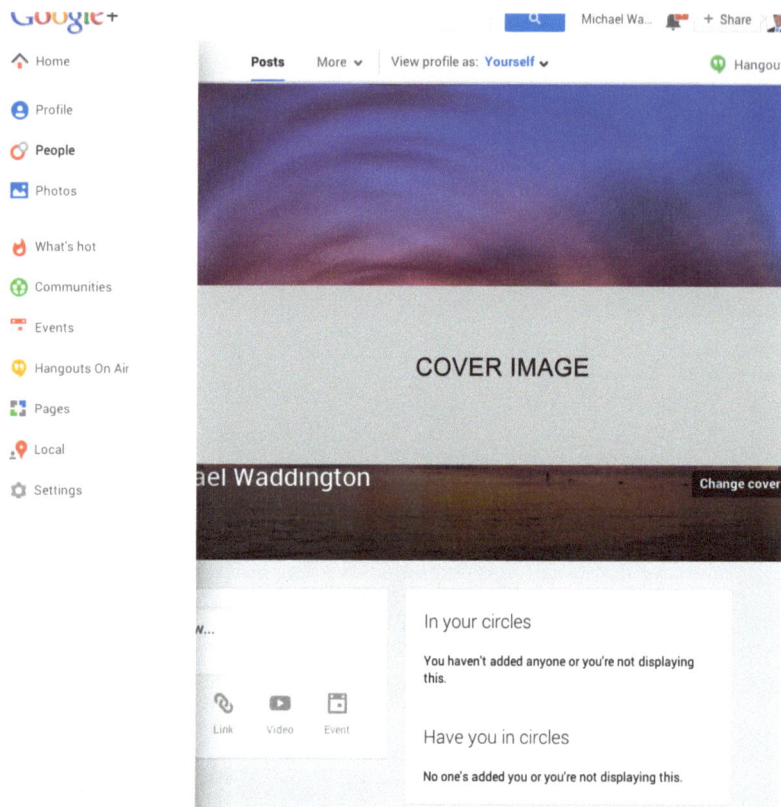

Figure 2.11: Get to the Find people screen

This brings you to the following page (see Figure 2.12):

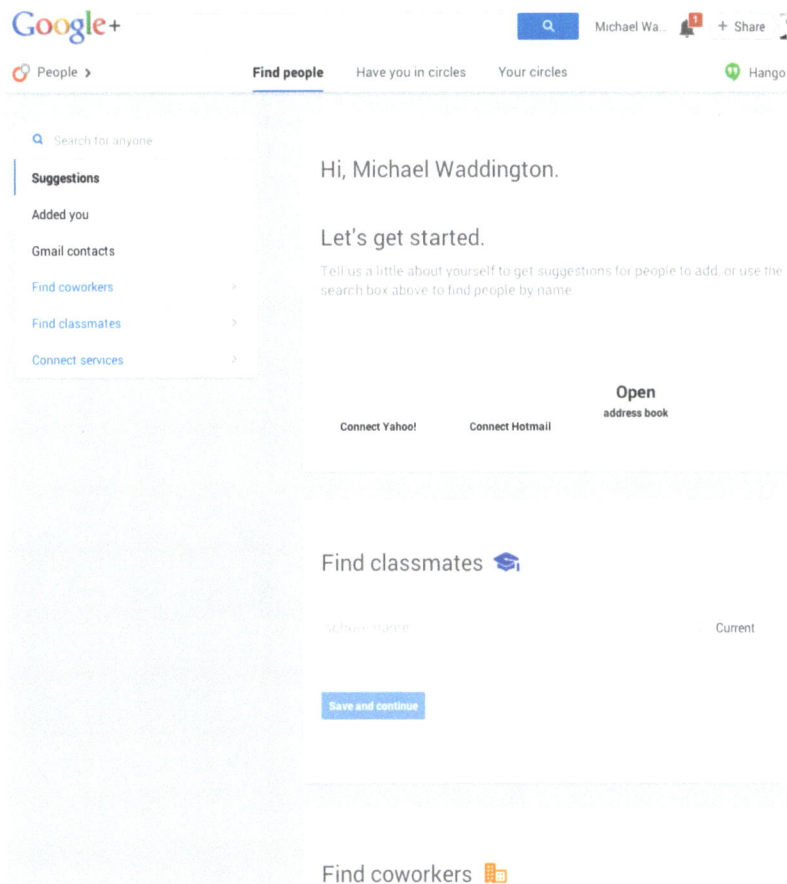

Figure 2.12: Find people screen

Once at this screen, click on your preferred service (Yahoo, Hotmail, etc.), or enter the company or school name you wish to search and click "Save and continue." The results are displayed on the next page and you can select the contacts you wish to add by clicking "Add" under their picture. We will cover Google+ Circles in another chapter.

Configuring "People" Settings

Next, you should configure the settings for the "People" section. From the "Find People" page, click on the "Profile" icon to the far left of your screen. This returns you to your profile page. The default view is "Posts." Click on "About" to the left of "Posts," both of which are found under your cover photo.

In the "People" section, you will see an "Edit" link. Click on it. You will see the following screen (see Figure 2.13):

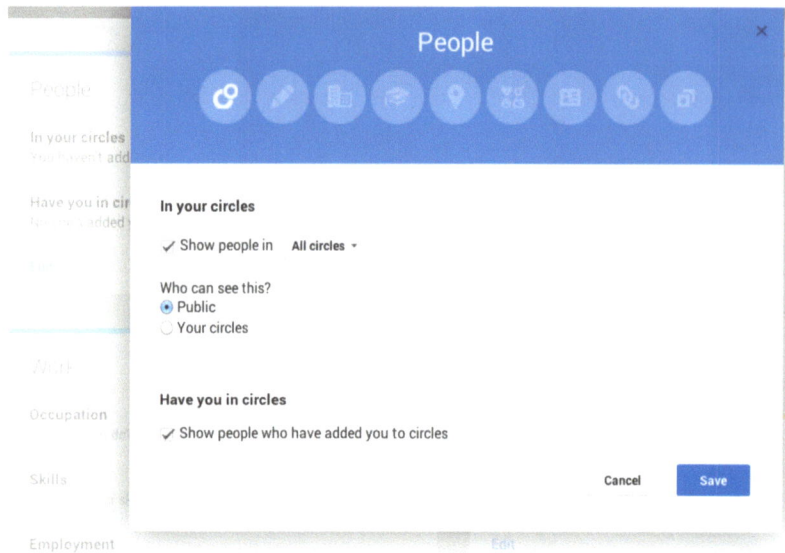

Figure 2.13: Edit People settings

Selecting How Your Circles are Displayed

You have a few options here. Under "In your circles" you'll see a checkbox next to the phrase "Show people in" and a drop-down menu titled "All circles." The choices available in the drop-down menu are: Acquaintances, Family, Following, Friends.

GOOGLE+ TIP

It is not necessary to have people in all four circles. For instance, if you are not planning to share or network with family members, then you may choose not to show that unused circle.

The results of these choices are displayed on your profile screen. If you uncheck the "Show people in" box, no one in any circle is displayed on your profile page. You are also given the choice of who can see people in your circles. You can allow your Circles to be viewed by the public or just those within your Circles. Below that, you may choose to show people who have added you to their Circles.

Setting Up Your Employment History

Next, click the "Edit" link under "Work" to bring up the following screen (see Figure 2.14):

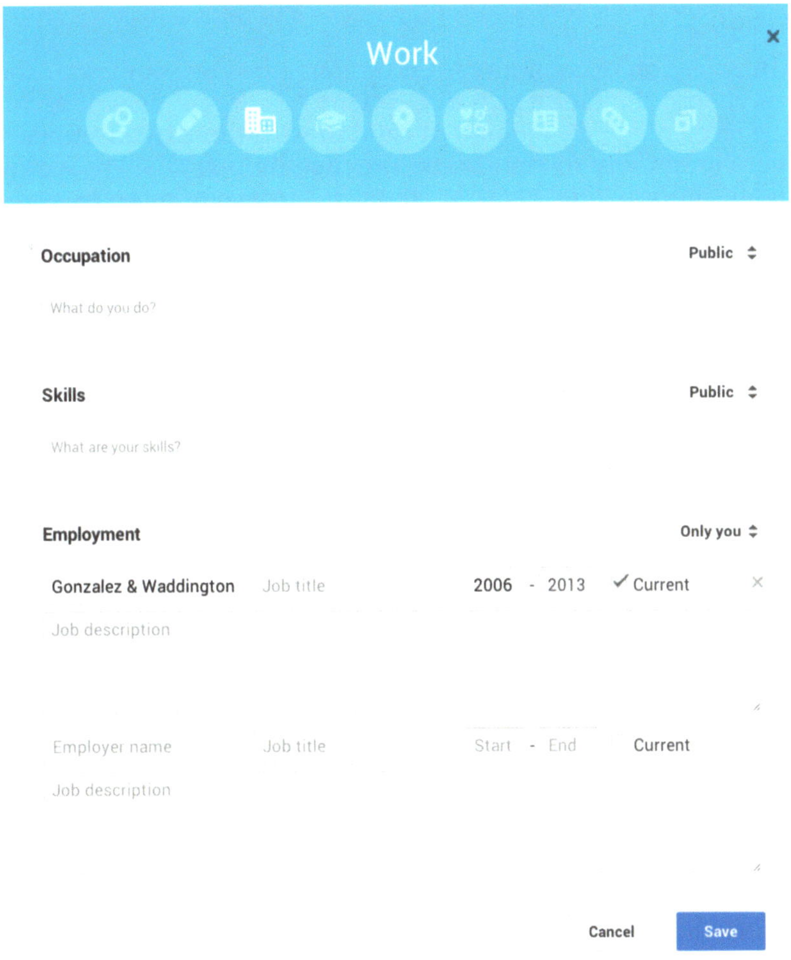

Figure 2.14: Work screen

Click on the individual boxes to fill in your responses. To the right of each question is a drop-down menu defaulted to "Public." The choices in this menu include: Extended Circles, Public, Your Circles, Only You, and Custom. This is one place in your profile where you should talk about what you do professionally. This is also one place where you may wish to choose "Public" as the setting. This allows your name to show up in search results when potential clients are searching for attorneys.

The other options in this menu require only a little explanation. "Extended Circles" allows people in your Circles and the people in their Circles to view your information. "Your Circles" and "Only You" are self-explanatory. "Custom" allows you to add people, Circles, and email addresses. Click "Save" when you are finished. This returns you to your profile page.

Places

The next section, "Places," is entirely optional. "Places" shows locations you have lived, in addition to your current city. As with the "Work" section, you can select who gets to view this information; the choices are the same as before.

Contact Information

The "Contact Information" section gives you options for how people can contact you at home or at work. You can choose the means, from telephone to address, as well as who gets to see this information. We suggest a moderate amount of caution with these two sections. Certainly, you will want to include your current city so you can be searched by that city. We highly recommend that you either leave home information blank or restrict it to your most trusted Circles. Entering contact information for your practice and making that publicly viewable should present no problem.

GOOGLE+ TIP

In Contact Information, you can insert your business address, phone, and email. It is not recommended to include your personal address, phone, and email unless you restrict access to close family members and friends.

Apps

The "Apps" section is for those who wish to use their Google ID to sign into other applications such as games, mobile apps, third-party websites, and online services without creating separate ID's for each one. At this point, however, we are not going to focus on this particular feature.

Story

This section allows you to tell the world a little bit about yourself (see Figure 2.15).

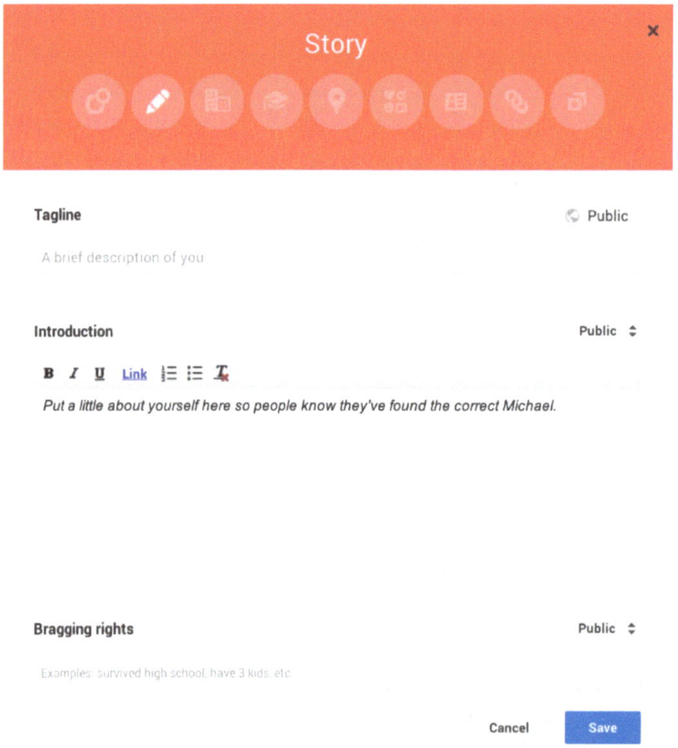

Figure 2.15: Story screen

Tagline

The first field is "Tagline," which asks for a brief self-description. Please note, the viewing setting for your tagline is public and that cannot be changed. We suggest taking this opportunity to promote your practice by entering a precise description. Below are a few examples of lawyer taglines.

"Experienced Los Angeles Divorce Lawyer"

"Atlanta GA Bankruptcy Lawyer"

"Dallas Criminal Defense Lawyer"

Introduction & Bragging Rights

The remaining two fields, "Introduction" and "Bragging Rights" ask for more specific information. You may choose to enter more information. However, we suggest that you keep it professional. Entering information about hobbies or sports is acceptable, as that shows you are a well-rounded individual. Avoid entering information dealing with political or religious affiliations and other "hot button" issues, unless these issues are somehow part of your practice. As with previous sections, you can select who sees this information. When finished, click "Save" to return to your profile page.

Here is a sample profile for a military defense lawyer.

Tagline:

Aggressive Military Defense Lawyer

Introduction:

Court Martial Lawyer - Military Attorney

Michael Waddington is a criminal defense lawyer that defends cases in military courts worldwide. He also defends military personnel that are under investigation and have not yet been charged. He specializes in defending serious criminal cases including sex crimes, war crimes, violent crimes, and white-collar crimes.

Gonzalez & Waddington, LLC

601 North Belair Square, Suite 16

Evans, GA 30809

706-664-1395

Visit our website www.ucmjdefense.com

Bragging rights:

Mr. Waddington has been reported on and quoted by hundreds of major media sources worldwide and has provided consultation services to CNN Investigative Reports, 60 Minutes, Katie Couric, ABC Nightline, the BBC, German Public Television, CNN, CBS, the 2010-212 Golden Globe winning TV series "The Good Wife" and other various international media outlets.

He appeared in a major CNN Documentary, the 2009 "Killings at the Canal" and some of his cases have been the subject of books and movies, including the Academy Award Winning Documentary "Taxi to the Dark Side" (view trailer), the 2013 documentary, "The Kill Team," the books "The 'Good Soldier' on Trial," "Strike & Destroy," and Brian De Palma's "Redacted," (De Palma also directed "Scarface" and "Carlito's Way").

In 2013, Mr. Waddington wrote a chapter in the American Bar Association (ABA) book, "The State of Criminal Justice 2013." This annual publication examines major issues, trends and significant changes in the criminal justice system and is one of the cornerstones of the ABA's Criminal Justice Section's work. This publication serves as an invaluable resource for policy-makers, academics, and students of the criminal justice system.

Education

In this section (see), you can enter all the schools you attended, from high school through law school. You can choose who sees this information by using the drop-down menu next to the text fields. We recommend, at a minimum, that you enter your undergraduate and law school information. Click "Save" to save this information and return to your profile page.

GOOGLE+ TIP

You should always include the official firm Name, Address, and Phone Number (NAP) in your Introduction. This will help your Local search engine rank.

GOOGLE+ TIP

Add a link to your website using your firm's official name, such as "Gonzalez & Waddington LLC."

GOOGLE+ TIP

Use these sections to provide as much information as possible about your firm and your services. Make sure to include your contact information, website address, and the geographic location(s) where you practice. You should also include keywords that relate to your practice areas, such as "criminal defense lawyer," "child custody attorney," etc. This will help your profile appear higher in Internet searches.

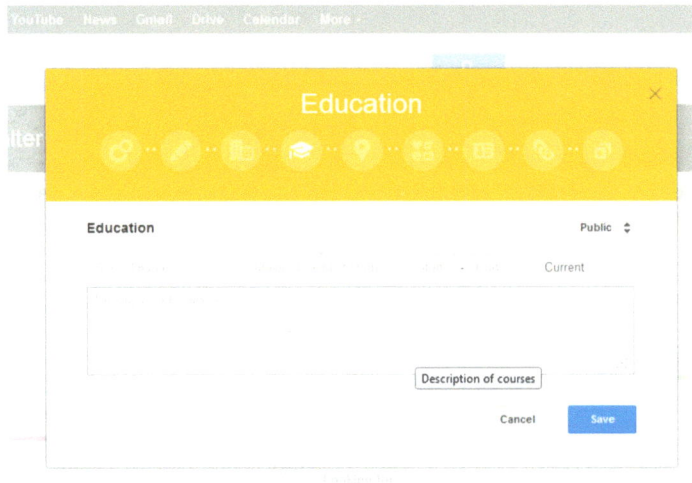

Figure 2.16: Education screen

Basic Information

The information requested in "Basic Information" (Figure 2.17) is information, such as gender, what types of connections you are seeking, your birthday, relationship status, and other given names or nicknames you are known by. Again, you are able to choose who sees this information in each category within the section. While this is your personal profile, required by Google in order to set up a Business Page, bear in mind that clients and potential clients may see this information. If you choose to add personal information, make sure to select appropriate security settings to control who views this information. It is generally safe to add your gender and birthday and allow it to be seen by everyone. You may also wish to include other names by which you may be known. For example, females that have married and taken their husband's name may want to list their maiden name. This helps clients who may be unaware of your name change find you.

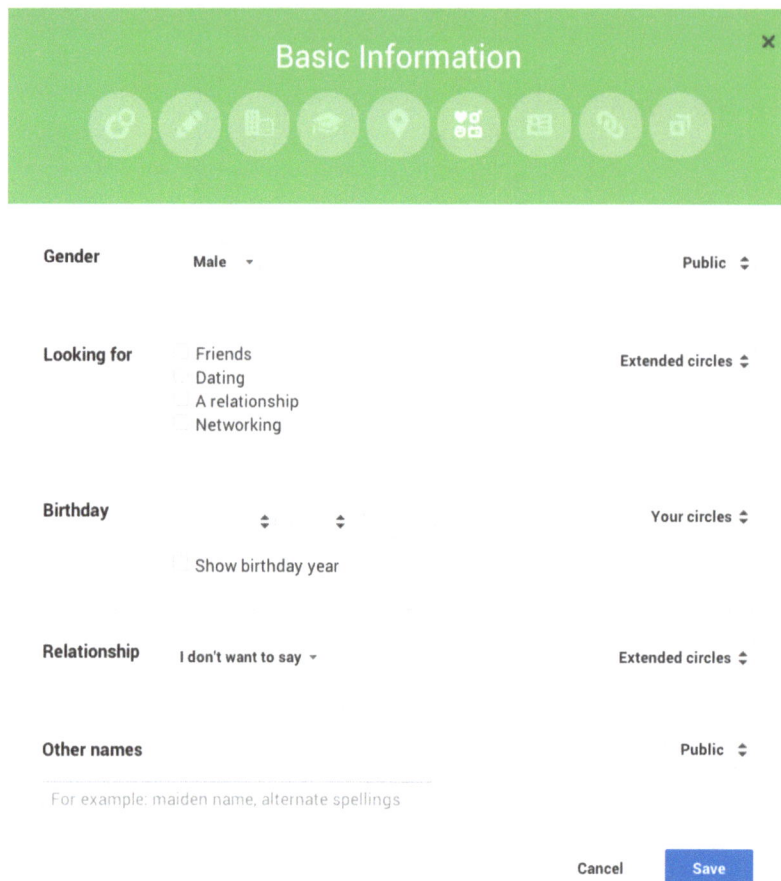

Figure 2.17: Basic Information screen

GOOGLE+ TIP

If you are going to allow information in the "Looking for" section to be viewed by the public, we suggest "Networking" only.

Links

This section (Figure 2.18) gives you the unique opportunity to link to your other profiles on systems such as LinkedIn and Avvo.com. You can also add links to sites that you contribute to. The latter is especially valuable if you have written articles for legal information websites. Lastly, there is an option to enter custom links to pages that may be of interest to you and your clients. A good suggestion is to link to the website of your local courthouse or other helpful sites related to your area of practice.

GOOGLE+ TIP

When adding other profile links, include as many of your firm's social media sites as possible. This will help build your overall authority on the Internet and also help with search engine optimization (SEO) and your firm's overall web presence. Lastly, remember to add links to your firm's website, YouTube channel, and blog.

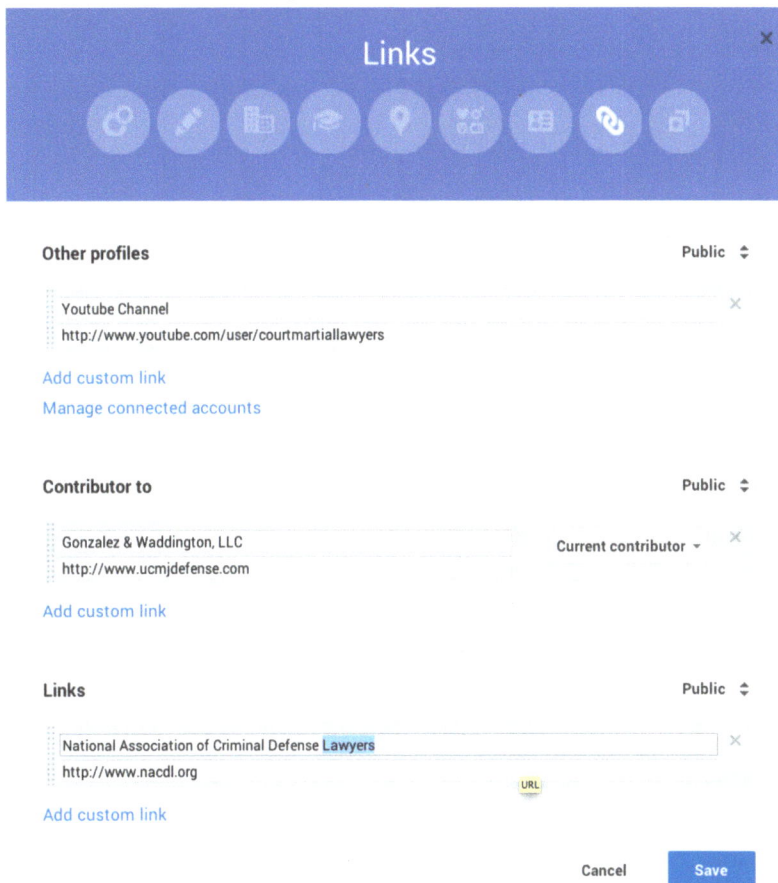

Figure 2.18: Links screen

Contributor To

You should add your firm website and blog to the "Contributor To" section. Later, when you connect your website and blog to your Google+ account, your photo will appear next to the search results on webpages to which you contribute (See Figure 2.19).

GOOGLE+ TIP

By linking your Google+ page to your website and vice versa, your photo will appear in search results. Studies show that people are more likely to click on a Google search result with an image next to it compared to a result without an image. Your photo will stand out and more people will visit your website.

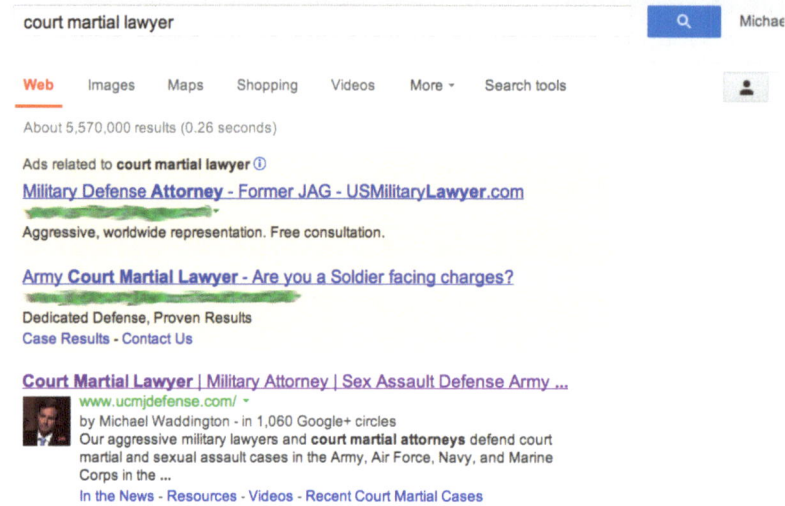

Figure 2.19: When a website is properly connected to a Google+ account, a Google+ profile picture appears next to the search result.

Other Links

If you choose to add links to other profiles, Google provides a preloaded list of options (see Figure 2.20). If the social media service you wish to add is not shown in the drop-down menu, click "Add custom link" and enter the requested information. Click "Save" to save the information and return to your profile page.

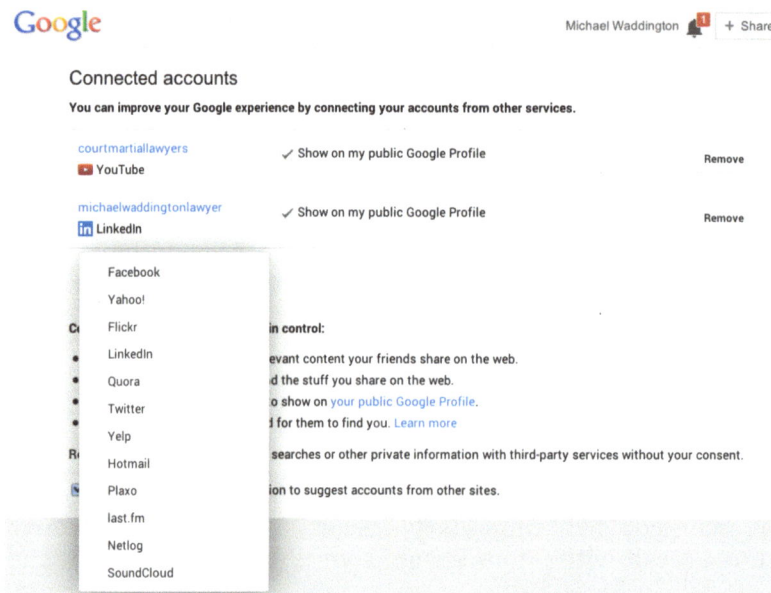

Figure 2.20: Pre–loaded list of services

Lawyers should add as many law-related social media links as possible. You should link directly to your social media profiles in the following legal websites: Avvo.com, HG.org, Lawyers.com, Martindale.com, lawyers.law.cornell.edu (Cornell Legal Directory), and http://lawyers.justia.com. If you do not have profiles in the above websites, then you should sign up immediately. These sites will help your local and organic search rankings.

Connecting Your Website to Google+

Lawyers should link their Google+ page to their website. This helps to increase your visibility in Google searches. It assists in connecting you with your colleagues, clients, and anyone else looking for your services online.

Linking the sites makes you eligible for Google+ Direct Connect. More importantly, according to the Google Support forum, linking sites "provides Google with information that we can use to help determine the relevancy of your site to a user query on Google Search." In other words: It helps your site rank higher in search results.

There are two ways to link your sites, Webmaster Linking and Direct Linking.

Connecting your website with your Google+ account is crucial to Internet marketing success. Shockingly, few lawyers do it. By linking your sites and leveraging the power of Google+, you will have a distinct advantage over your competitors that do not connect their sites. Based on Internet searches conducted while writing this book, it appears that only a small percentage of lawyers, in cities across the US, have properly connected their Google+ account with their website. If your Internet marketing company has not done this, then you need to seriously consider hiring a different company. Connecting your website to Google+ gives you an edge over your competition.

Webmaster Tools Linking

If your website is verified with Google Webmaster Tools (http://google.com/webmasters/tools), then you can use Webmaster Tools to link your Google+ page with your website. If you do not have a Webmaster Tools account, then use the Direct Linking method (described in the next section) or sign up for an account at the link above.

To connect your website to your Google+ page, follow these steps:

1. Login to your Google+ account.

2. Click on your Profile icon, on the left of the screen.

3. You will see the "About" tab. Click "Link website," located next to your website address.

4. If you have access to your Webmaster Tool, then login and confirm the link request.

5. If you do not have access to Google Webmaster Tools, then contact the person that has access to your Webmaster Tools (typically your web designer, SEO company, or webmaster).

When the link is approved, you will be notified by email. Or, you can verify the connection by logging in to your Google+ account and clicking on the "About" tab on your profile page. If your website is connected, you will see a checkmark next to your website address.

Additional resources for Google Webmaster Linking:
https://support.google.com/plus/answer/answer.py?answer=1713328

Direct Linking

You can directly connect your Google+ page with your website. To do this, you need to insert a short snippet of code into your website. If you are unfamiliar with how to edit your website code or do not have access to the code, then seek expert assistance or use the Webmaster Linking method.

To use the Direct Linking method, follow these steps:

1. Make sure your website appears in Google search results. You can do this by entering the following text into the Google search bar: "site:yourwebsite.com" (Note: replace "yourwebsite.com" with your website address). If your site does not appear, then seek the advice of an SEO or Internet marketing professional.

2. Get your Google+ page ID number. To do this, go to your Google+ page and look at the website address. It should look similar to this: https://plus.google.com/123456789. The number after ".com/" (i.e. 123456789), is your Google+ page ID. You will need this number to connect your website to Google+.

3. Modify the following code by replacing "**yourpageID**" with your Google+ page ID mentioned above.

   <a href="https://plus.google.com/**yourpageID**"

   rel="publisher">Find us on Google+</a>

4. The modified code should look like this:

   <a href="https://plus.google.com/**123456789**"

   rel="publisher">Find us on Google+</a>

   (Note: Make sure the number matches YOUR Google+ page ID).

5. Add the above modified code to your website code. You should add the code to your sidebar or footer. This links your website to your Google+ page. (Note: This code must be added to the website code and not pasted into the website text).

6. Next, modify the following code by replacing "**yourpageID**" with your Google+ page ID mentioned above.

   <link href="https://plus.google.com/**yourpageID**" rel="publisher" />

7. The modified code should look like this:

<link href="https://plus.google.com/**123456789**" rel="publisher" />

(Note: Make sure the number matches YOUR Google+ page ID).

8. Add the above modified code to your website's <head> tag.

9. Now, login to your Google+ account.

10. Click on your Profile icon, located on the left of the screen.

11. You will see the "About" tab. Click "Link website," located next to your website address.

12. Follow the instructions in the box that appears:

    a. On your Google+ page, click "Test."

    b. Google will check to see if you properly inserted the code into your website.

    c. If your website is properly connected, then you should see a checkmark within the next 24-72 hours.

13. If the checkmark does not appear after a few days, then visit https://support.google.com/webmasters/bin/answer.py?hl=en&answer=1708844 for more details on this topic or seek professional assistance.

Additional resources for Google Direct Connect:

http://support.google.com/plus/bin/answer.py?hl=en&answer=1711199

https://support.google.com/plus/answer/answer.py?answer=1713328

Optimizing Account Settings

Before moving forward, let's take a moment to optimize your account settings. It is wise to optimize your account at the beginning. Otherwise, you may later discover that you have shared something you did not intend to share. From your profile page, go to the upper right hand corner and click on your picture. Then, click on the "Account" link. This takes you to the Account Overview page (see Figure 2.21).

From this page, you can change your recovery email address (used if you have lost your login credentials), change the language in which your profile is displayed, and review and upgrade your data storage plan. Google gives every user 5 GB of free storage. If at some point you decide to stop using Google, you can delete your account, and all information associated with it, from this page as well.

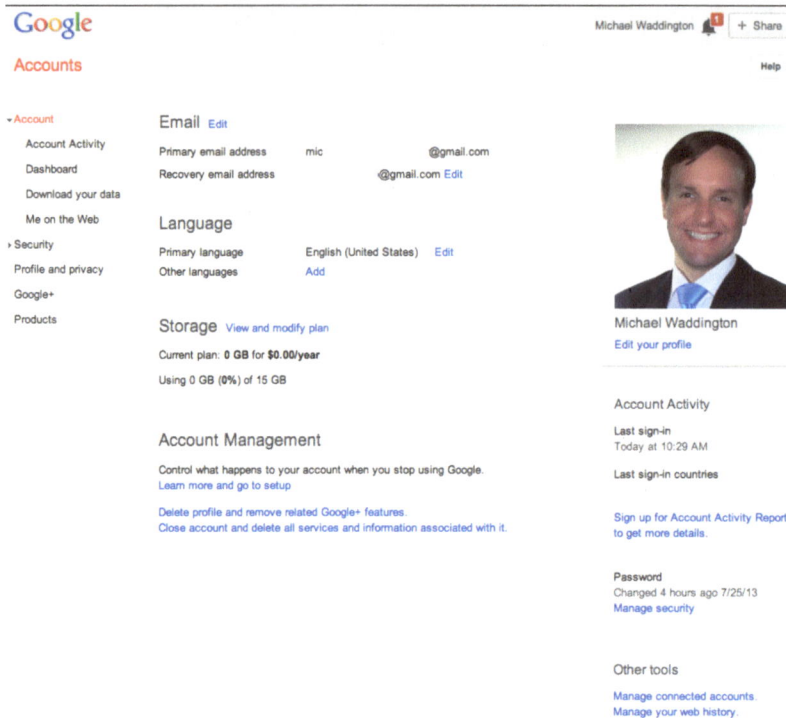

Figure 2.21: Account Overview screen

Account Activity

Along the left side of this page, you will notice a variety of selections listed under "Account." The first three links, "Account Activity, Download Your Data, Me on the Web," are part of your account settings. The other four are links to security and privacy settings that we'll cover in the next section. Click on "Account Activity," which opens the following page (see Figure 2.22):

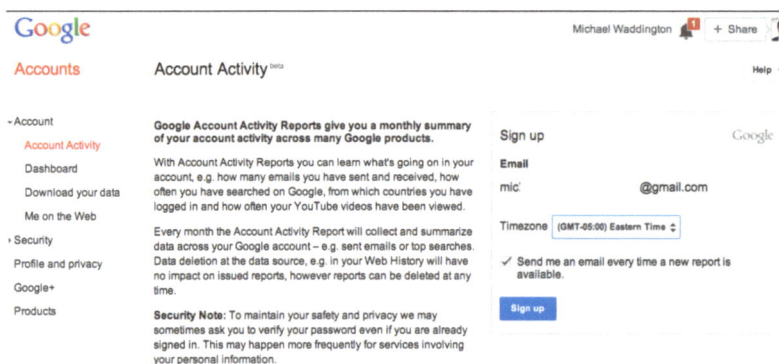

Figure 2.22: Account Activity sign-up

This is an optional service. You must sign up in order to use it. This allows Google to send you monthly summaries of how many emails you send and receive, how many Google searches you conduct, and how often your YouTube videos have been viewed. This latter item becomes important from a marketing perspective in a later chapter. In short, if you are posting brief webinars (and you should be), knowing how often they are viewed is a metric allowing you to assess the effectiveness of this marketing tool. If you find, for instance, that you are not getting many views, then you may want to change how you promote your webinars. This topic will be covered in greater detail in a later chapter.

Download Your Data

The next item, "Download Your Data," allows you to back up your Google+ information to your computer. Regular backups should be conducted to ensure the safety of your information. Web photo albums, profile information, contacts, and Circles are among the information that is downloadable (see Figure 2.23).

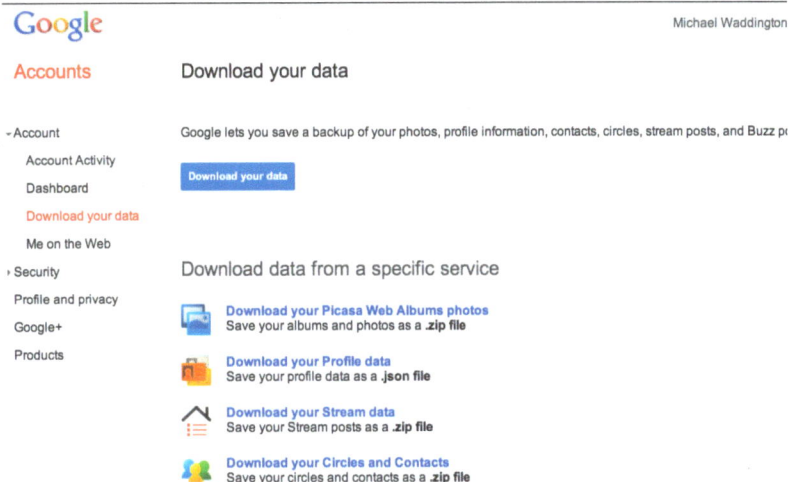

Figure 2.23: Download you data screen

Me on the Web

The final item under accounts is "Me on the Web" (see Figure 2.24). This is a suite of three handy services valuable to business owners. The first, "Search for Yourself," allows you to see what others see when they search for you on Google.

The second, "Stay Current with Web Alerts," allows you to receive email from Google when information about you appears online, such as your name in a Google search result.

The third and final tool, "Review Your Google+ Profile," is a reminder to keep your profile current. As with any online presence, your Google+ information should be kept as current as possible, not only for the sake of accuracy, but because it is important to marketing your business. Clients and potential clients who notice out-of-date information on your Google+ pages may wonder if you have gone out of business.

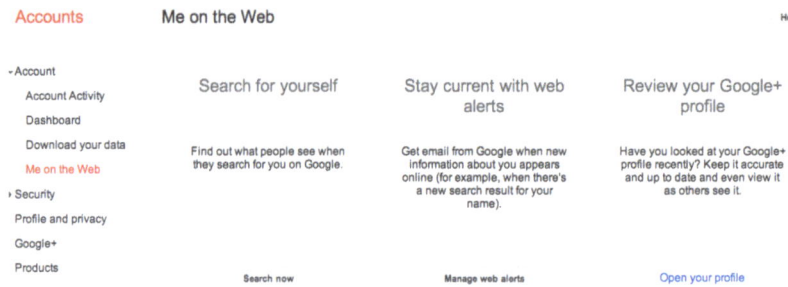

Figure 2.24: Me on the Web screen

Optimizing Security Settings

This screen allows you to perform a number of security-related functions. You can change your password, update your recovery options, sign up for 2-Step verification, and manage notifications, as well as your connected applications and sites. Of these options, the 2-Step verification and connected applications are the ones that require further explanation.

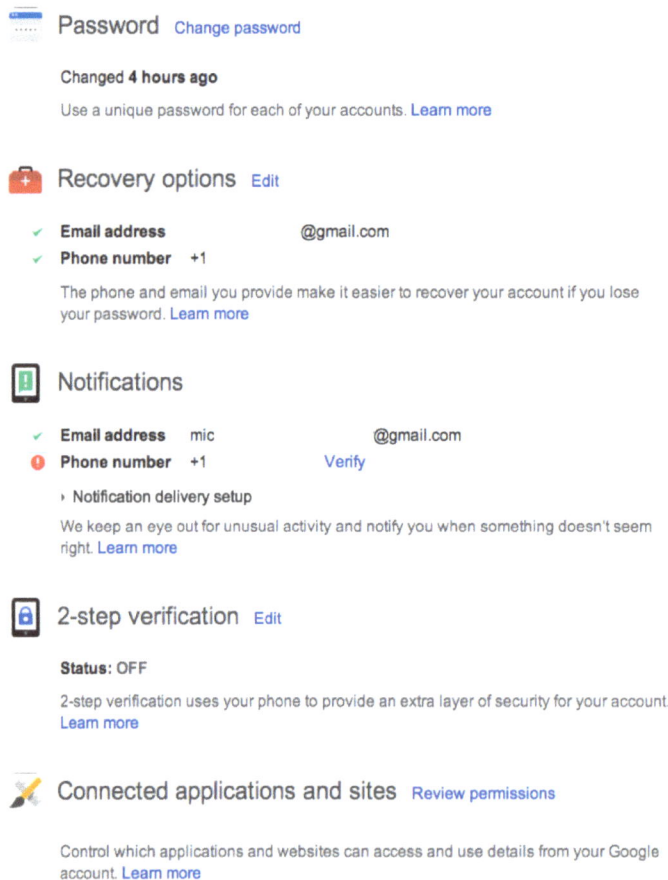

Figure 2.25: Security settings

2-Step Verification

2-Step verification adds an additional layer of security to your Google+ account. Signing up for this service means an authorization code will be sent to the phone of your choice each time you log into your account. The rationale behind this service is to prevent unauthorized users from accessing your account from unauthorized computers. In the settings for this feature, you can authorize your computer to ask for your password and not a verification code upon login. You are still protected, as any user attempting to login from a different computer will be asked for a verification code that they will not be able to provide.

In the screenshot above (see Figure 2.25), this feature is turned off. To activate it, click on "Settings" next to the feature name. On the following page, click on "Start Set up." You will be asked to enter the phone number you would like your verification code sent to, and the format in which you would like to receive it, either text message (SMS) or voice call. Do so and click "Send Code." If you have chosen to receive your authorization codes by text message, you will receive a six-digit code shortly thereafter, typically within a few seconds. If you choose voice call, then you will receive an automated call with the code in about the same time frame. Enter the code and click "Verify Phone."

GOOGLE+ TIP

You should use your cell phone to verify your account. If you happen to get locked out of your account, which is likely at some point, it is easier to unlock the account using a cell phone rather than an office phone, particularly if you are on vacation, it is after hours, or on the weekends when you may not be in the office.

Since it's possible you may lose your phone at some point, it's strongly advised that you create a trusted computer from which you can access your account without a verification code. We suggest a computer that is used only by you, or by you and people you absolutely trust. If the computer you are using to set up this account is a trusted computer, check that box and click "Next." You can always change the designated trusted computer later.

Click on "Confirm" in the next screen. You will be asked for your password to complete the process. Please enter it and sign in again. This takes you to the following page (see Figure 2.26):

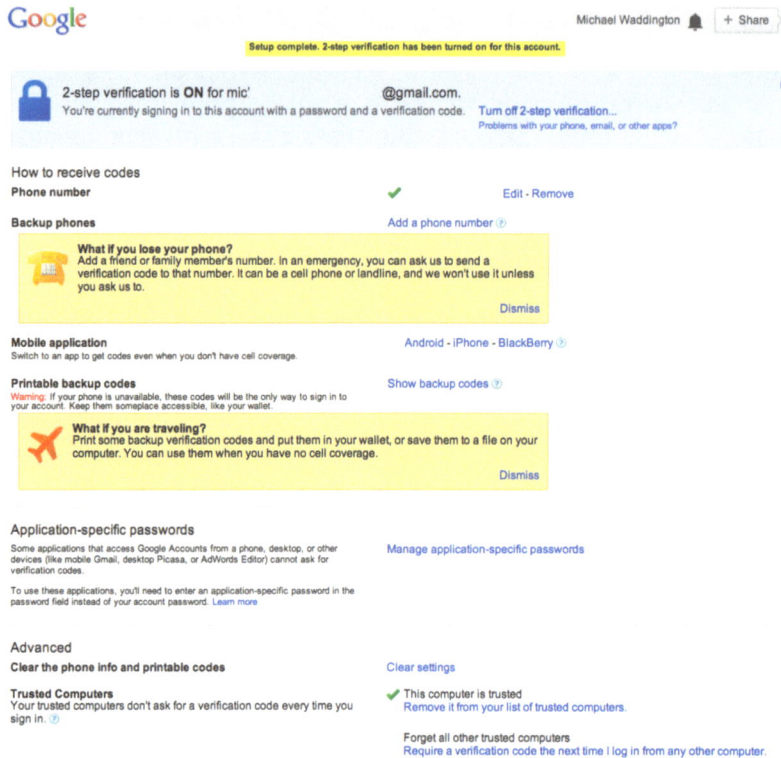

Figure 2.26: How to receive codes

Receiving Password Recovery Codes

This screen shows various backup methods of receiving codes. You can assign an alternate phone number to a friend or family member. If you are traveling with the possibility of no cell coverage, you can print a list of backup codes. You can also manage application-specific passwords and clear your phone, printable codes, and trusted computers if you need to change them.

Connected Applications and Sites

The last security setting to optimize is "Connected Applications and Sites." Click on "Manage Access."

Since you have not yet set up any sites or applications, this area is blank. You can always return to it if you wish to set up connected sites or apps. It is important to note not all applications that work outside a browser work with 2-Step verification. Applications such as Microsoft Outlook™, chat clients (AIM™, Google Talk™, etc.), and applications running on smartphones (Android™, BlackBerry™, iPhone™, etc.) cannot ask for verification codes. You can set up application-specific passwords, though. As this is a means of simplifying access to applications that may be more focused on personal use, we will not explore this feature here. Google+ provides a video tutorial if you are interested in using this feature.

Optimizing Privacy Settings

There are two methods of accessing your Google+ privacy settings. One is by clicking on "Privacy" from your profile picture in the upper right corner (see Figure 2.27).

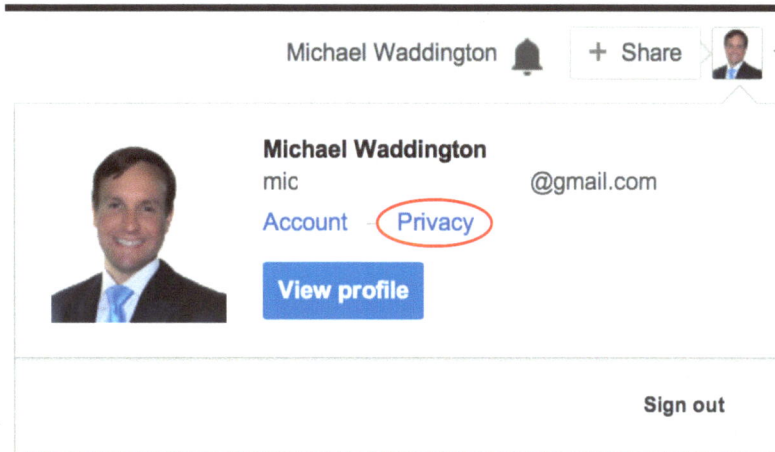

Figure 2.27: One method of accessing privacy settings

Another way is clicking on "Profile and Privacy" on the left side of the account settings page (see Figure 2.28).

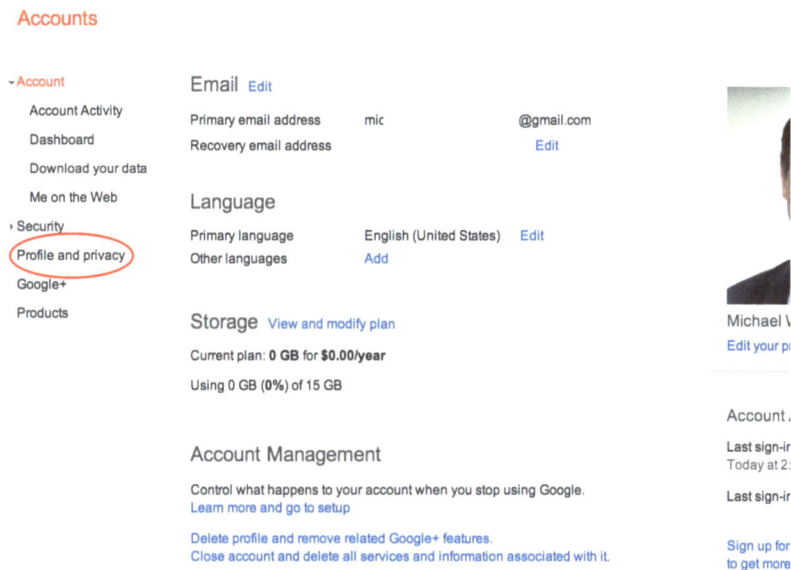

Figure 2.28: Second method of accessing privacy settings

Both methods take you to the same page, as shown below (see Figure 2.29):

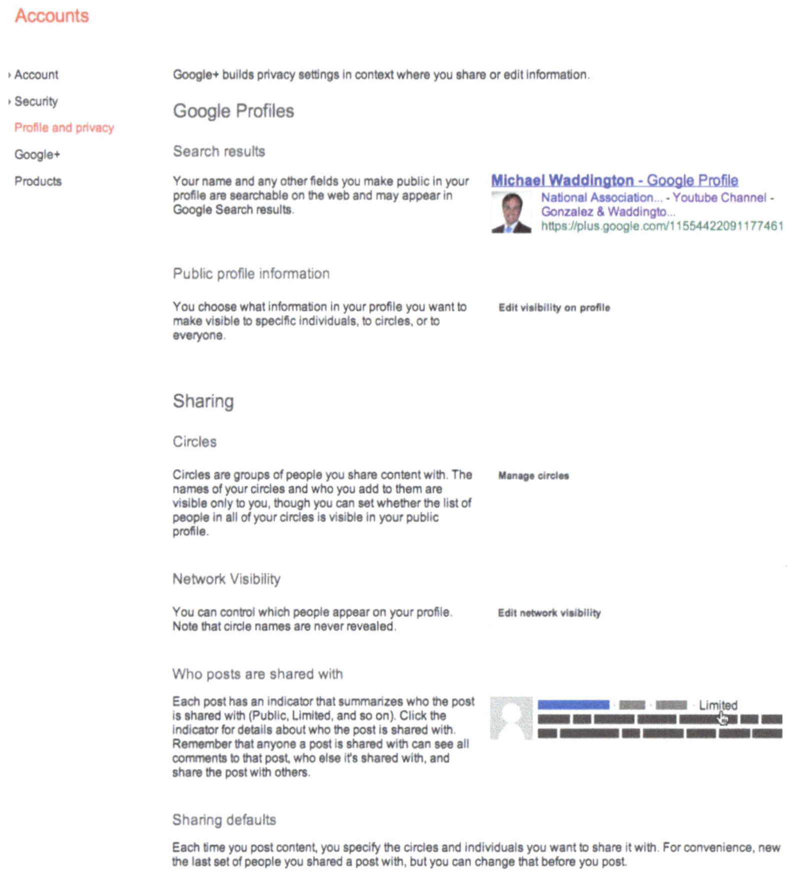

Figure 2.29: Privacy settings page

There is a lot to cover on this page, however, some of it will be familiar since it was done during your initial profile setup. Starting from the top down, let us begin with "Google Profiles."

Google+ Profile Privacy

Search results: You will see your profile photo and a link. The link takes you to a public view of your profile. Any information you make public appears in search results.

- Public profile information: Click on the "Edit visibility on profile" link to choose who gets to see what information.

NOTE: You did this in the various sections (People, Work, etc.) when you set up your profile initially. This is where you come if you want to change those settings. They can also be changed from the "About" page of your profile by clicking "Edit" in the individual sections.

Circles Privacy

Circles: There is a separate chapter devoted to the subject of Circles so we will not cover that here.

Network Visibility Settings: This controls which people are visible on your profile, e.g., your connections.

NOTE: This screen is the same as the "People" section mentioned above in "Google Profiles" and can be accessed here or from the "About" page of your profile. The names of your circles themselves (Family, Friends, Clients, etc.) are never revealed to anyone.

Posts Sharing and Privacy

These settings control who can see your posts. This is done on a post-by-post basis (see Figure 2.30). A later chapter covers "Posts" in greater detail.

The Posts default is to share with whoever you selected to see your last post, so be careful! Before you post content, double check and make sure it is being shared with your intended audience. You can change who will see your individual posts before you click "Share."

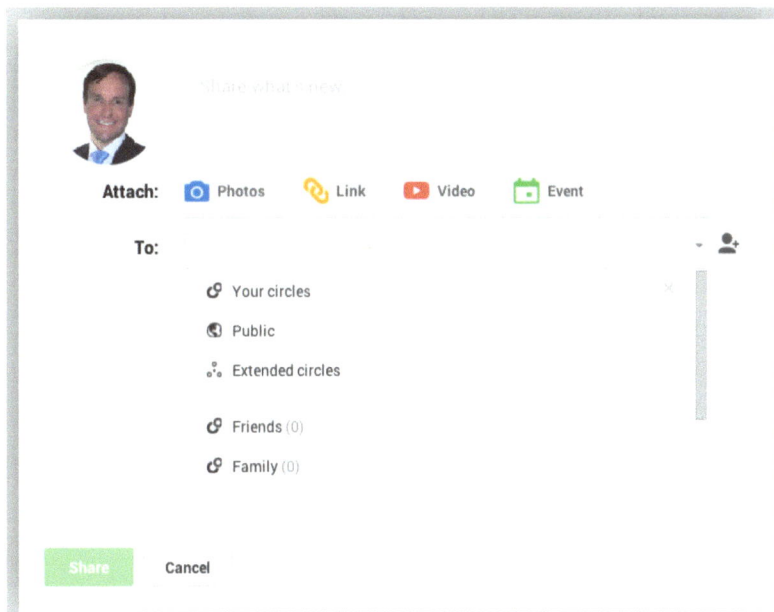

Figure 2.30: Post settings

Photo Sharing and Privacy

Photo Sharing Settings: This allows you to control how your photos are seen. Click "Edit photo settings" to access the settings. You can access photo settings here, but you also have access to other Google+ settings that are covered under the "Google+" link at the side of the page. We will cover photo settings first, then move on to the others.

Tagging is a way of identifying people in photos. For example, if a family member on Google+ posts a photo of a family dinner and tags you in the photo, then anyone who views the photo can scroll over your face and see your name.

Every time you are tagged in a photo, you will receive a notification. You can either approve the tag or remove it.

Location allows you to attach the location where the photo was taken as you upload them.

Photos tab: This setting lets you decide whether you want a visible "Photos" tab on your profile page.

Photo Settings (see Figure 2.31):

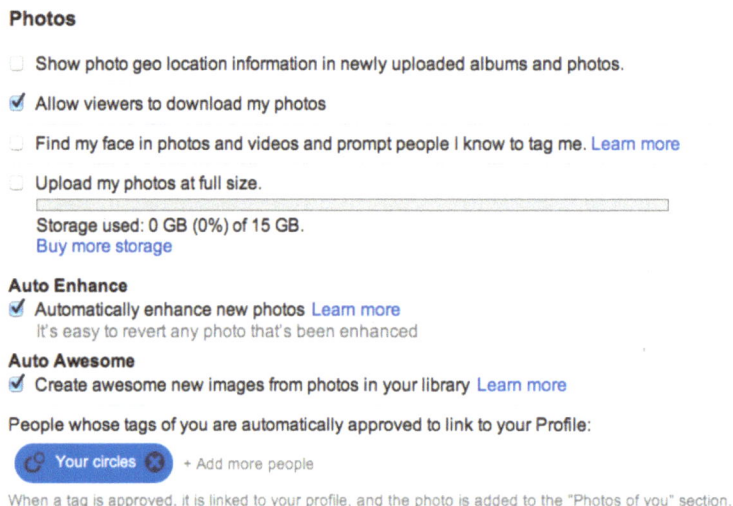

Photos

☐ Show photo geo location information in newly uploaded albums and photos.

☑ Allow viewers to download my photos

☐ Find my face in photos and videos and prompt people I know to tag me. Learn more

☐ Upload my photos at full size.

Storage used: 0 GB (0%) of 15 GB.
Buy more storage

Auto Enhance
☑ Automatically enhance new photos Learn more
It's easy to revert any photo that's been enhanced

Auto Awesome
☑ Create awesome new images from photos in your library Learn more

People whose tags of you are automatically approved to link to your Profile:

[Your circles ⊗] + Add more people

When a tag is approved, it is linked to your profile, and the photo is added to the "Photos of you" section.

Figure 2.31: Photo settings

Geo Location Information

Geo location information allows the geographic location of photos you upload to be identified. We have no recommendation as to the optimal setting, unless you are uploading photos taken in places you would prefer not to identify.

GOOGLE+ TIP

If you are uploading professional images of you, your firm, or your city, then you should geo tag the images with your firm's official name, address, and phone number.

Allow Viewers to Download my Photos

This setting allows whoever sees your photos to download them. Google+ defaults to "Allow." We recommend that you deselect this option. While you may want to allow certain Circles (Family, for instance) to download the photos they're allowed to see, this setting is very broad.

For example, you might select "Allow downloads" because you want to allow family to download family photos. Therefore, anyone who can view your Family Album can download those photos. The public cannot download these photos because they cannot see that album.

Just keep in mind that all of your albums can be downloaded by those with permission to view them. For example, your Friends Circle can download any photos in your Friends Album and Clients can download photos (if any) in your Clients Circle, etc.

Why be concerned? As lawyers, you are familiar with how photos affect people in positive, as well as negative ways. At the topmost level of concern, if a photo can be downloaded, it can be repurposed or used by whoever downloads it, thus violating your property rights in the photo. In addition, we occasionally have conflicts with those close to us.

Say you have a photo of yourself in your Friends Album of a night at the bar acting foolish, and you later have a "falling out" with a friend in your Friends Circle. Months or years later, you are in a hotly contested race for Juvenile Court Judge. This embarrassing photo could be downloaded and posted in more public forums, causing you professional embarrassment.

It is better to field requests from Circle members for copies of photos, thus allowing you to make the final decision, than it is to let everyone download whatever photos they can access at their security level.

Upload My Photos at Full Size

This allows you to upload your photos in their full, uncompressed format. If you are uploading images, then you should be aware of your storage limitations. You get 5 GB of free storage space. Uploading photos at full size will take up a lot of space. However, know that you can always purchase more space if you need it.

Photo Tagging - Find My Face and Prompt People I Know to Tag Me

This setting uses Google's face recognition ability to create a model of your face. When you, or someone you know, views a photo of you, you get a notification prompting you to tag – or approve someone else's tag – of your photo. You can reject tags from others, if you wish.

Tag suggestions do not alter sharing settings of photos or albums. However, when a tag suggestion is approved, the person tagged is able to see the photo and the album in which the photo is stored. Again, be wary of who sees which photos.

People whose tags of you are automatically approved to link to your Profile allows you to choose the people, Circles, or email addresses of those whose tags of you automatically approve.

These tagged photos are linked to your Profile and added to the "Photos of You" section located in your albums. Click in the add field to make your selection. As with all photo settings, we advise caution in putting "tags" on automatic. Manually approving or rejecting tags is the preferred way to manage tags.

NOTE: You can change the settings at any time from the appropriate page.

Managing Photo Albums

To manage photo albums, go to your Profile and click on Photos. From there, click on "View all" next to "Your Shared Albums" (see Figure 2.32).

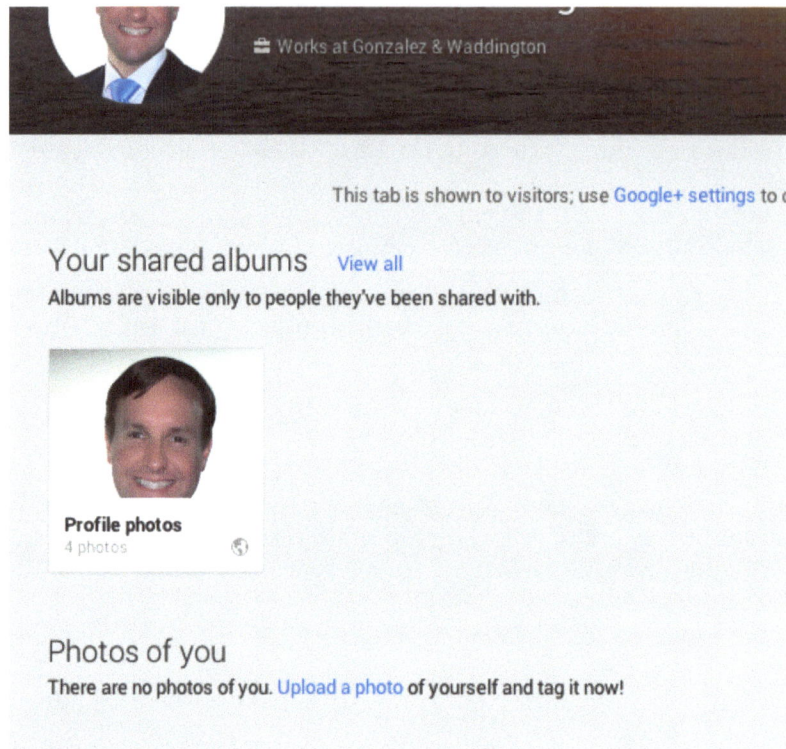

Figure 2.32: Accessing albums

Album Sharing Settings

From this screen, you can select who sees your various albums. Each album's settings are handled individually via drop down menu. You have the choices of "Public, Extended Circles, Your Circles, Limited, and Only You." The only option we haven't addressed before is "Limited." This option allows you to add Circles, email addresses, and specific individuals to each album.

You can also lock or unlock your albums. The default setting is unlocked. Locking prevents the re-sharing, tagging, and linking to and commenting on a photo in a "+Share" post. Depending on what other shared settings you've designated, you may wish to lock it, especially if you do not want photos tagged. This means you will not get tag requests on the photos in this particular album since the photos are locked and cannot be tagged.

Note: You already learned the basics of photo uploading when you set up your Profile. We will cover album creation and uploading to specific albums in a later chapter.

The last "Profile and Privacy" settings we will cover deal with the Dashboard and Privacy Center. These items are located directly below Hangouts on the Profile and Privacy Settings page (see Figure 2.33).

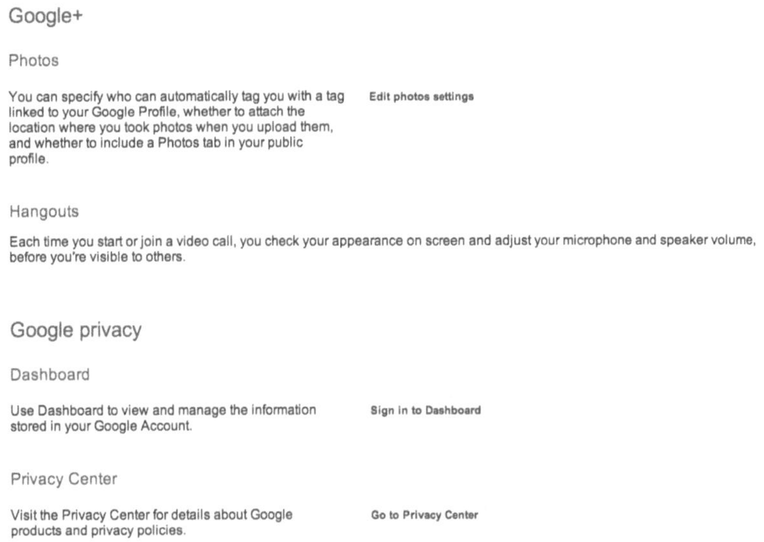

Google+

Photos

You can specify who can automatically tag you with a tag   Edit photos settings
linked to your Google Profile, whether to attach the
location where you took photos when you upload them,
and whether to include a Photos tab in your public
profile.

Hangouts

Each time you start or join a video call, you check your appearance on screen and adjust your microphone and speaker volume,
before you're visible to others.

Google privacy

Dashboard

Use Dashboard to view and manage the information   Sign in to Dashboard
stored in your Google Account.

Privacy Center

Visit the Privacy Center for details about Google   Go to Privacy Center
products and privacy policies.

Figure 2.33: Google Privacy settings

Google Privacy settings

These items are not really settings, however, they are important and contain information you should be familiar with. Dashboard is actually more of an overall management area that allows you to manage aspects of your Google+ account. We will cover Dashboard in greater detail when we teach you how Google+ can be used as a tool to grow your practice.

The Privacy Center is an informational page that explains Google's privacy policies. The following is taken directly from that page:

Our Privacy Policy explains:

• What information we collect and why we collect it.

• How we use that information.

• The choices we offer, including how to access and update information.

The last settings we will cover are accessed by clicking on the links below the "Profile and Privacy" link. Earlier, when covering the photo settings found under the "Google+/Photos/Edit photo settings" link, you were introduced to other settings, too. These can be accessed either by the link already mentioned or by clicking on the "Google+" link at the side of the page (see Figure 2.34).

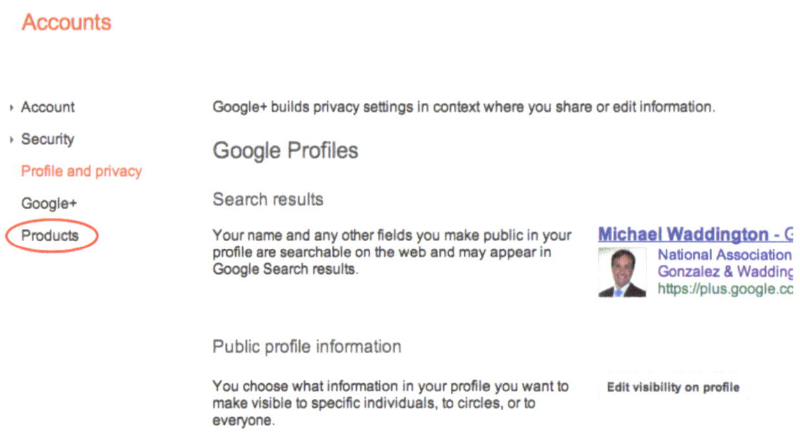

Figure 2.34: Google+ and Products links

Clicking on the Google+ link, circled in red above, takes you to a page that is long enough to be reminiscent of the first time you saw a chart of the Federal Rules of Civil Procedure as a law student. For ease of use, we have broken the screenshots down into sections.

The first section deals with who can interact with you and your posts (see Figure 2.35). You can choose who can send you notifications (types of notifications are in one of the next sections) and who can comment on your public posts (the posts you allow everyone to see). This is a matter of preference. However, we suggest allowing everyone to send you notifications. It's a means of tracking your presence on Google+, which is a valuable metric when we get into marketing your practice in a later chapter.

We also suggest you allow everyone to comment on your public posts. Remember, you are trying to attract new clients; your posts are a way of getting your practice noticed. A prospective client may see a public post about a topic in your practice area and ask you a question about it. You can begin a conversation with this person by asking them to email, call, or visit your office for a consultation.

Notification Delivery

Below that, you will see "Notification delivery." This shows the email address where your notifications are sent. You can change the address or add more addresses. It also gives you the opportunity to receive notifications via text message. We recommend against the latter as you may find the volume of texts to be cost-prohibitive or just plain annoying.

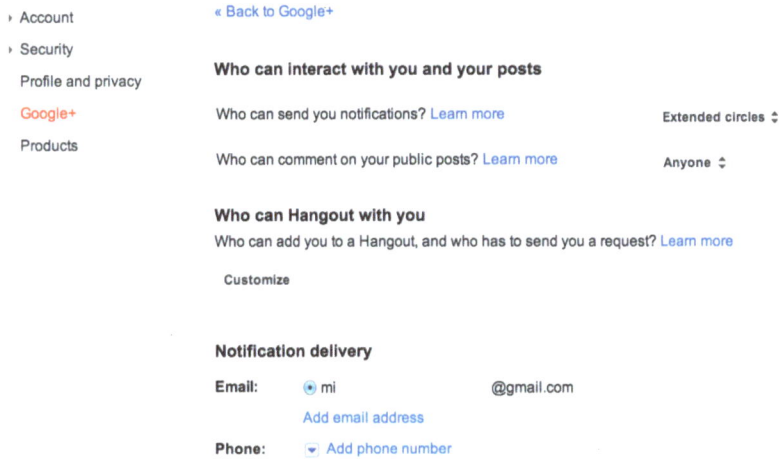

Figure 2.35: Interaction with posts and Notification delivery

Managing Subscriptions

The next setting deals with "Managing subscriptions" (see Figure 2.36). These two settings allow occasional updates about Google+ activity, friend suggestions, and updates from people outside your Circles. There may be some value here in that Google+ can notify you of potential networking partners. However, if you choose to allow these updates, monitor them to make sure they are worth your valuable time. The default setting is to allow them. Uncheck the boxes if you want to stop receiving them.

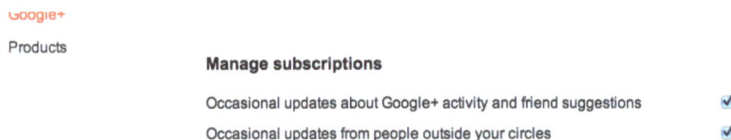

Figure 2.36: Managing subscriptions

Types of Notifications

Now, let's look at the types of notifications you can receive (see Figure 2.37). If you chose to receive notifications by email, that is reflected in the screenshot by the envelope and the word "email" along the right side of the page at each heading. The default setting is that you receive notifications for everything. If you do not want to receive certain notifications, then uncheck the box next to that notification type.

Receive notifications

Notify me by email or SMS when someone...

Posts	Email
Mentions me in a post	☑
Shares a post with me directly	☑
Shares a post and they're in a circle I subscribe to	☑
Comments on a post I created	☑
Comments on a post after I comment on it	☑
Circles	Email
Adds me to a circle	☑
Suggests new people to add to my circles	☑
Joins who is in my contacts	☑
Photos	Email
Tags me in a photo	☑
Tags one of my photos	☑
Suggests a profile photo for me	☑
Comments on a photo after I comment on it	☑
Comments on a photo I am tagged in	☑
Messenger	Email
Starts a conversation with me	☑
Hangouts	Email
Invites me to a video call	☑
Starts a new Hangout with me	☑
Events	Email
Invitations or updates to events	☑
Reminders about events I'm invited to	☑
Activity on events I created	☑
Communications about Pages	Email

Figure 2.37: Notification types

This may seem like a long list, but it's easy to manage. We recommend that most of the notification types remain checked. For Posts and Circles, it's a matter of marketing. You will receive notifications when someone mentions you, shares something with you, comments on one of your posts, or comments on a post after you comment on it. This keeps you in the know about how you are being perceived on Google+; it also allows you to interact with potential clients and colleagues who comment on your public posts.

Photo notifications should be left on so that you are made aware of being tagged, as well as for comments on photos you post. Again, it's a metric that allows you to evaluate your presence and reach on Google+.

Receiving Messenger, Hangouts, and Events notifications provides you a convenient reminder of things in which you may want to participate.

Notifications of Communication about Pages and Communities keeps you abreast of networking opportunities. Communication about Pages allows you to receive invitations to manage Pages, including communities or groups in which you are involved. Community notifications give you a heads-up when someone invites you to become a member of a community on Google+.

Games, Apps, and Circles

The next section deals with Games, Apps, and Circles (see Figure 2.38).

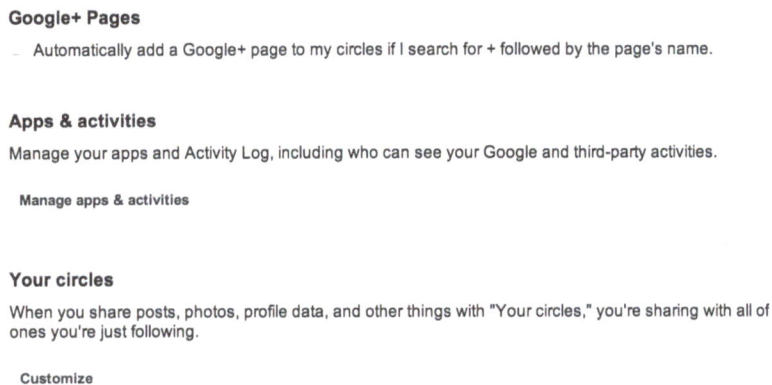

Google+ Pages

Automatically add a Google+ page to my circles if I search for + followed by the page's name.

Apps & activities

Manage your apps and Activity Log, including who can see your Google and third-party activities.

Manage apps & activities

Your circles

When you share posts, photos, profile data, and other things with "Your circles," you're sharing with all of ones you're just following.

Customize

Figure 2.38: Games, Apps, and Circles settings

This is a straightforward section. The Google+ Pages setting (default is "No") automatically adds a Google+ Page – be it a business, person, or group – to your Circles if you search for it by entering "+ the page's name" in your search. Searches are covered in detail in the next chapter. We suggest leaving it set as "No" (unchecked); otherwise, you will spend valuable time de-cluttering your Circles.

Google+ Games shows notifications of any Google+ Games you play in the Google Bar. The Google Bar appears at the top of every Google page (if you are signed in) and looks like this (see Figure 2.39):

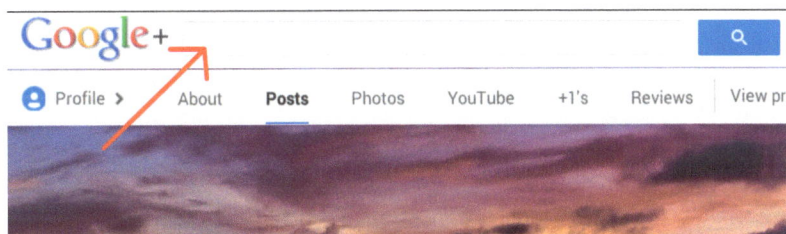

Figure 2.39: The Google Bar

The default for showing your Google+ Games (a topic not covered in this book) is to show them. Only the number of notifications shows, not their topics. If you play any Google+ Games, particularly any that send notifications, this could become distracting since you will not know if it's a potential client commenting on a post or a friend posting a new high score on a game. We suggest unchecking it purely from a productivity point of view.

The Apps setting allows you to manage any apps you sign in to using your Google+ ID. As this feature is not a focus of this book, we will not cover it here. Customizing your Circles is the next setting. However, a full chapter is dedicated to Circles so we will cover it there.

The final settings of this section are shown in the next screenshot (see Figure 2.40).

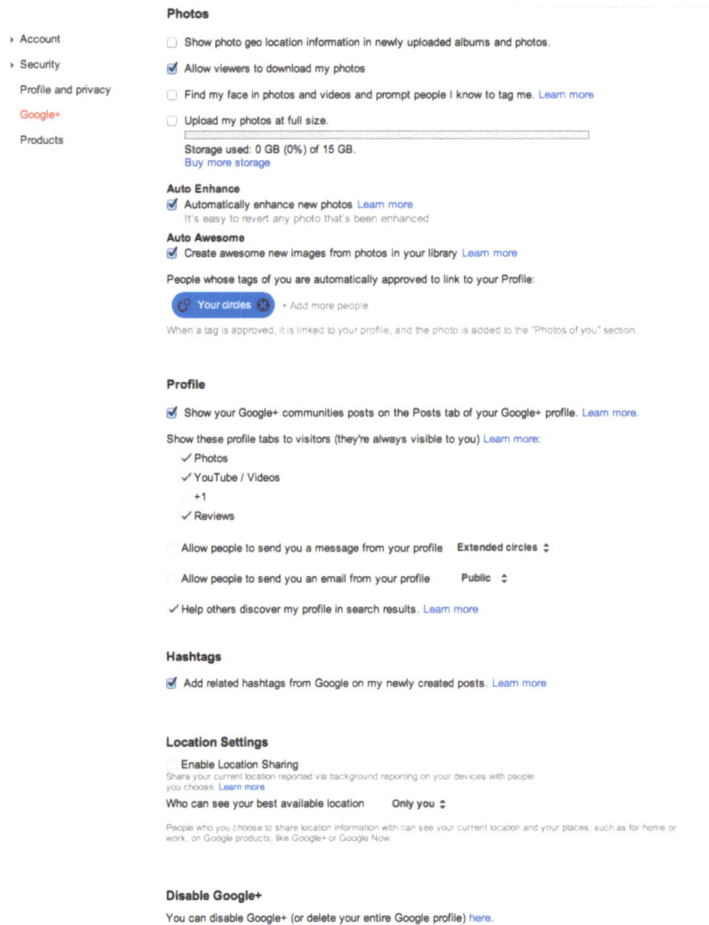

Figure 2.40: Photo, Profile, Location, and Disable settings

Photo, Profile, Location, and Disable settings

The Profile settings allow you to further refine who sees what content on your Profile page. The defaults are shown above. You can choose whether posts from Google+ communities you belong to are displayed on your profile page.

NOTE: These posts are viewable only by other members of the same community unless that community's setting is "public."

The next Profile setting deals with which tabs are visible to visitors (About, Posts, Photos, Videos, +1's, and Reviews). All of these are always visible to you. Next, you can choose whether to allow people to message you or email you from your Profile page, as well as which people can do so. Last is the setting that helps others locate your Profile in search results.

Given that this book's primary focus is teaching you how to use your Google+ account to expand your practice, we suggest using the default settings. This allows others to see you are a lawyer, without giving them access to irrelevant personal information. They can contact you from your practice page, which we will set up later. You could allow the "+1" tab to be visible if you are judicious as to the things you "+1" (remember, the "+1" is the Google+ version of Facebook's™ "Like").

Location Sharing

We suggest you leave Location Sharing turned off. There is no professional advantage to having your every move tracked and broadcast, even if you can choose who sees the information.

Deleting Your Google Account

This setting is available if you decide to abandon either Google+ or all Google products. You can delete your Google+ content, in which case Google attempts to restore your remaining Google products to their pre-Google+ state, or you can delete your entire Google profile. The latter removes not only your Google+ account and content, but also Gmail and all other Google products you access with that profile ID and password. Be advised: Neither option is reversible. If you do either and later change your mind, you will have to start all over again.

The final setting for this chapter involves Google Products (see Figure 2.41). Clicking on "Edit" gives you the opportunity to remove the listed products or delete your entire account. Signing in to your Dashboard gives you another means of managing this information.

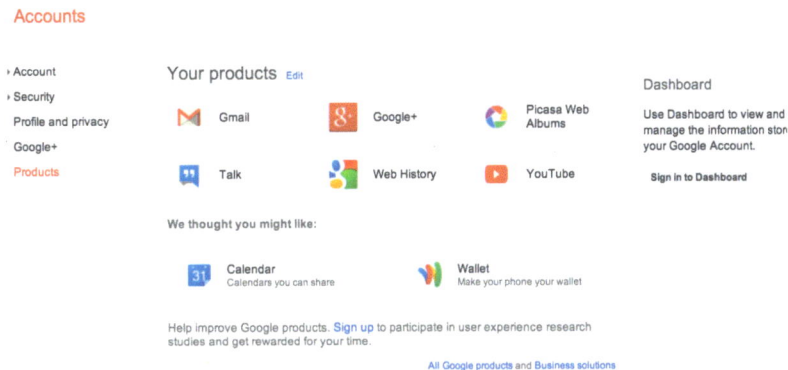

Figure 2.41: Google products

Chapter 3: Navigating Google+

Now that you have set up a profile and optimized all of your settings, it's time to learn your way around Google+. There are a few different ways of searching out people, businesses, and communities. This chapter shows you how to use each method, as well as how to connect to those you find through your searches. A later chapter covers all the ways you can maximize these connections to expand your practice.

The Google+ Search Bar

The first method, the Search Bar, is the easiest method. It's found at the top of every page under the menu bar. Do not confuse it with the address bar at the very top of the page. The Google+ search bar is directly to the right of the Google+ logo.

You can search for people by entering names, or portions of names. Once entered, click on the magnifying glass to the right of your entry. The results appear below the Search Bar (see Figure 3.1).

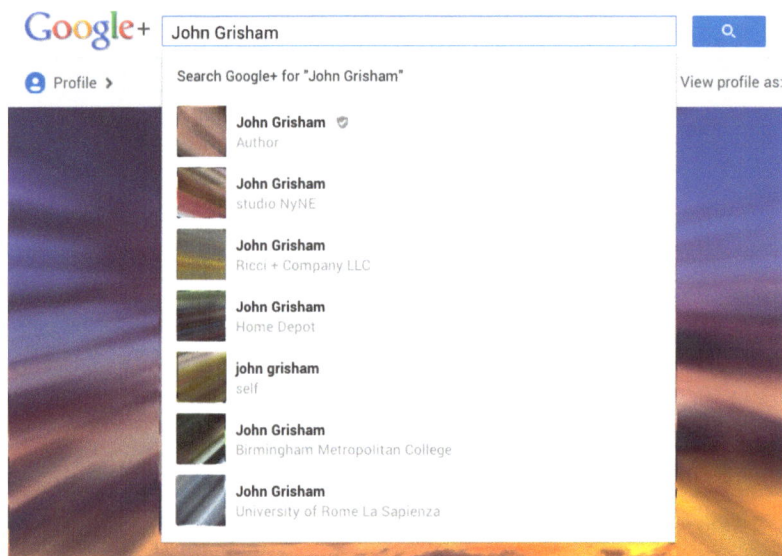

Figure 3.1: People search results

Click on the person you wish to see and you are taken to their Google+ Page. This also works for finding businesses and communities. The steps are the same, only you enter a business name such as "Google," or a description of a community you may wish to join, such as "personal injury lawyers." As with people, the results are displayed below the Search Bar (see Figure 3.2).

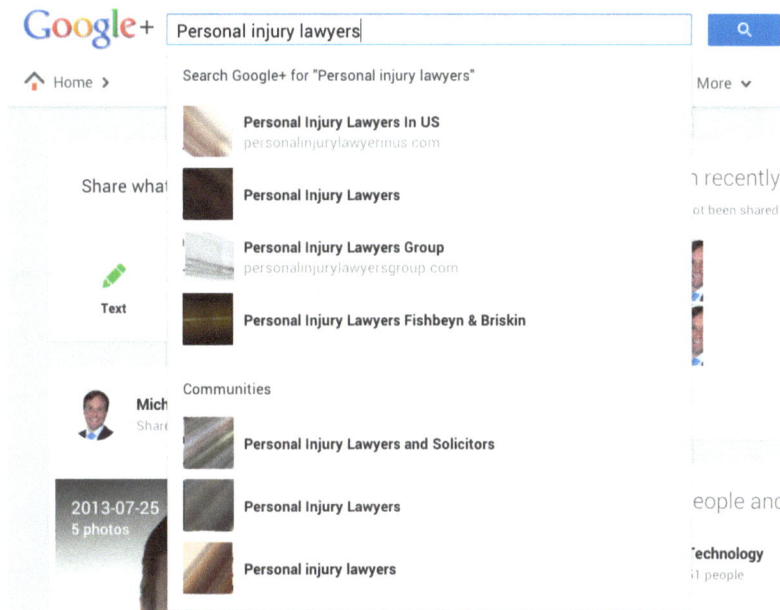

Figure 3.2: Community search results

This is one way to find the people, businesses, and communities you seek. You can make invaluable connections, as well as tap into a great knowledge base.

People Searches

This option is also easy to use. To begin, you have to select the "People" option from the menu (see Figure 3.3).

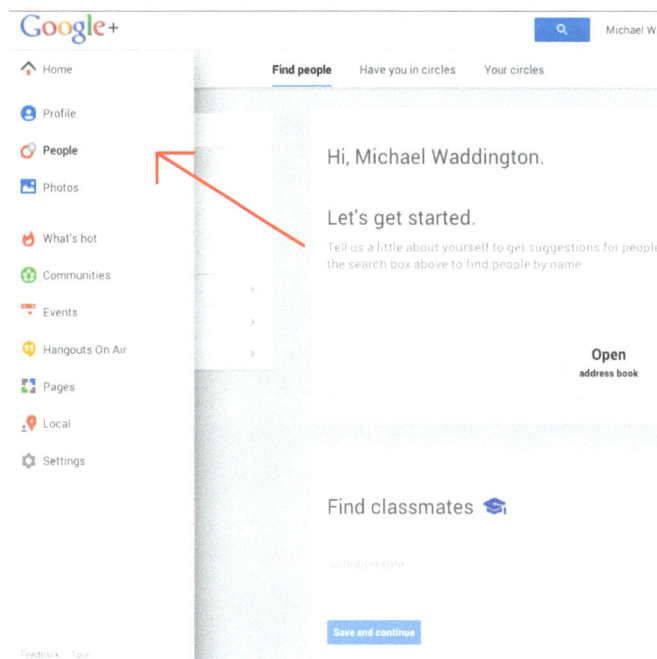

Figure 3.3: Select "People" from the menu

This takes you to the following search screen (see Figure 3.4)

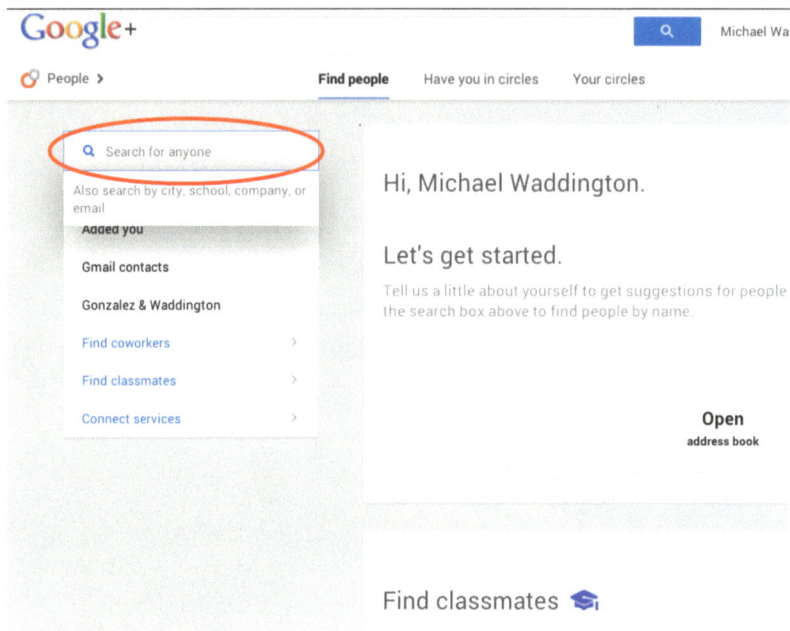

Figure 3.4: People search screen

Type your search into the "Search for anyone" box. Results will display below the search (see Figure 3.5).

Figure 3.5: People search results

If you want a complete listing of results, hit "enter" after typing your search query. This returns a comprehensive list of results (see Figure 3.6). As before, click on the person whose page you wish to see.

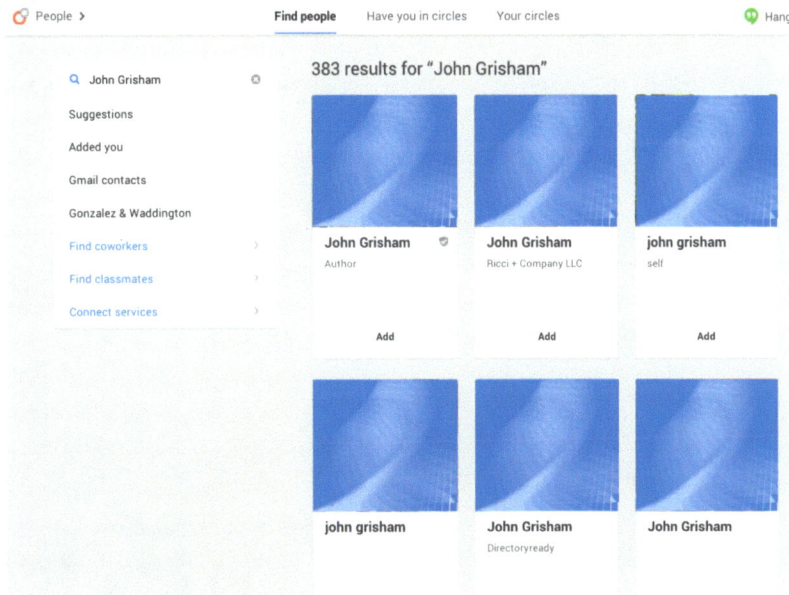

Figure 3.6: Expanded search results for People

GOOGLE+ TIP

The People search does more than just find individuals. You can also find businesses and communities using this search tool.

Community Searches

Google+ Communities are groups of like-minded individuals and businesses joined together for the common purpose of sharing knowledge and networking. Let us take a look at finding Communities.

Just as you did for "People," select "Communities" from the menu at the left of your screen (see Figure 3.7).

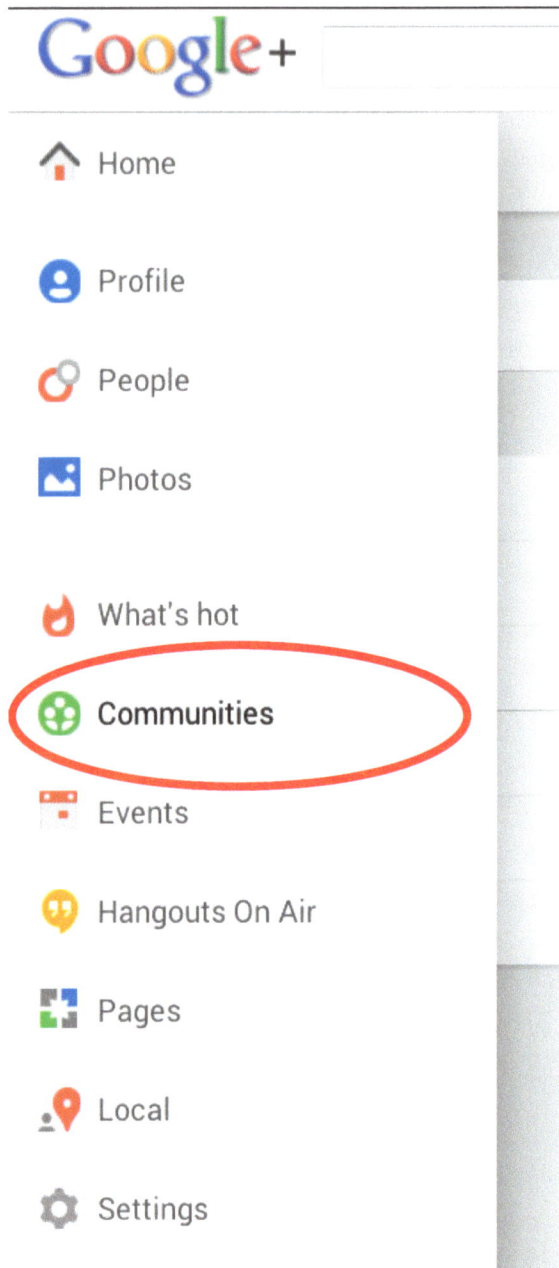

Figure 3.7: Communities menu

This takes you to the "Communities" screen. As you can see, Google+ gives you a preselected group of Communities. Clicking on any of them takes you to that Community's Page. Feel free to explore personal interests on your own; for now, we will stick to Communities of interest as an attorney, that could potentially benefit your practice.

There is a "Search" box at the upper right of the Communities screen (see Figure 3.8). You will also see a "Create community" button; we will cover that in a later chapter.

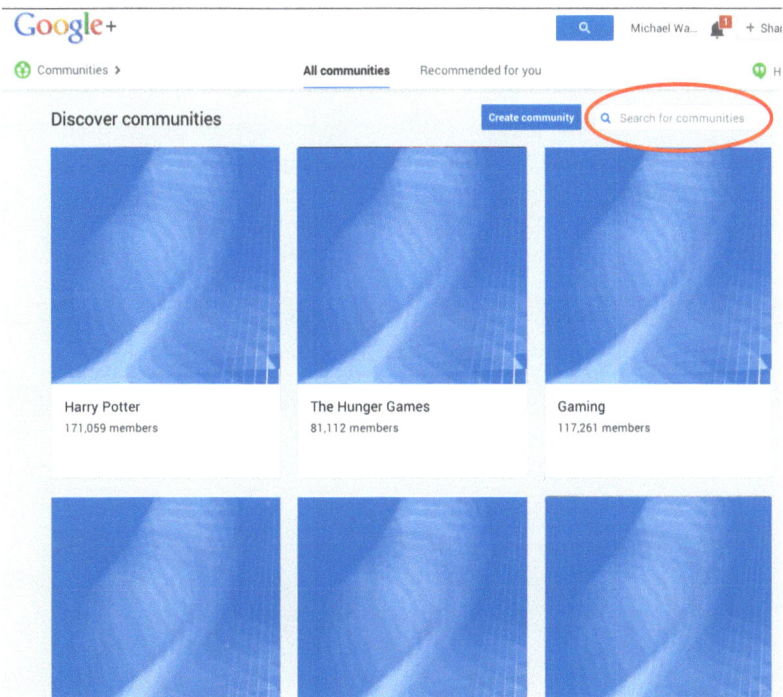

Figure 3.8: Search for communities

If you want to find Communities catering to personal injury attorneys, then type "personal injury" into the "Search for communities" box and hit "enter." This takes you to a new page offering several choices (see Figure 3.9). Click on a particular Community to see its Page.

GOOGLE+ TIP

Try to join well-established, active communities with a decent amount of members and posts. If you want to network with other lawyers, it does you no good to join a community with few members and no posts.

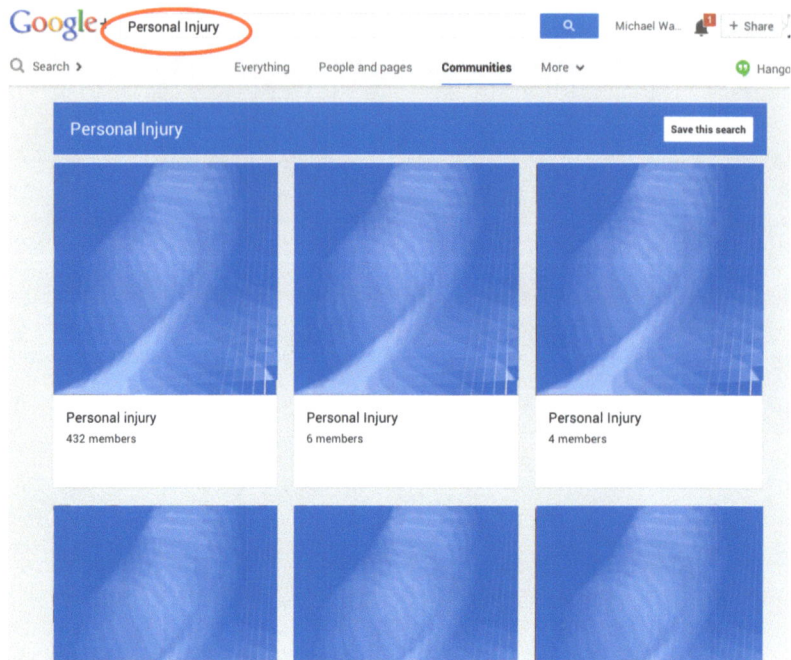

Figure 3.9: Results of Community search

What's Hot Searches

This is the final method of searching. While this method is interesting and goes a long way towards keeping you abreast of trends and breaking news, it is quite general. It is a form of searching where you may find items of interest (some of them may even be law-related); however, there aren't options to narrow the search here.

Under Hot Searches there are suggested Communities and Interesting People and Pages. You also get the Trending box at the upper right. Here, you find timely topics currently trending on various media outlets. Clicking on any topic takes you directly to that specific page.

How Searching Helps Your Practice

Searching helps your practice by uniting you with like-minded people (lawyers), businesses, and Google+ Communities. These are all sources of new contacts, as well as potential business. Anything that gets you out there – and noticed – is a good thing. Marketing is all about developing a presence. Networking with other attorneys and joining Communities sets you up for three important possibilities:s

1. Referrals. Case-overloaded practitioners can use Communities, and trusted individuals, for assistance when their caseloads become overwhelming. You can get those referrals. Likewise, you can ask for help if your caseload occasionally gets out of hand.

2. Knowledge base. There are times when you have a unique question or need a sample motion or other court document. Take it to your Communities or trusted Circles; chances are great

that someone can help you. You might even end up helping someone else. That kind of cooperation goes a long way towards building a strong network.

3. Clients! This is what we all want: More business. There are Communities on Google+ for potential clients seeking legal advice. It may not be a good idea to publicly answer the legal question in their post, but by clicking on the poster's name, you are taken to their Google+ page. Now, you can engage them in a conversation, potentially becoming their attorney.

Chapter 4: Google+ Circles

In previous chapters, we have mentioned Google+ Circles. Now, we are going to learn what Circles are and what they can do for you.

While Google+ Communities are akin to traditional forums designed around a central theme, like "Star Trek," or "vintage Ford cars," Circles are much more intimate. Unlike Communities, which are controlled by a moderator, you control your Circles.

Google+ Circles mimics the way we interact with others in "real life." This is equally true when it comes to expanding your practice. As you use Google+ to widen your professional networking system, find clients, keep clients informed on issues of importance, and also keep up with family and friends, you do not want everyone to know everything.

Sharing photos of your daughter's 12th birthday party with criminal clients or showing your trust and estate clients' images of your sister's bachelorette party in Las Vegas is not appropriate. Likewise, your friends likely do not want to be bombarded with updates on estate planning, and your family probably does not care about mass tort reform. Where it is difficult to make sure these necessary divisions occur on other social networking sites, Google+ Circles makes it easy.

Setting Up Your Circles

First, click on the "People" menu, as you did when searching. Then, click on "Your Circles" in the upper middle of the page. This takes you to your Circles page (see Figure 4.1).

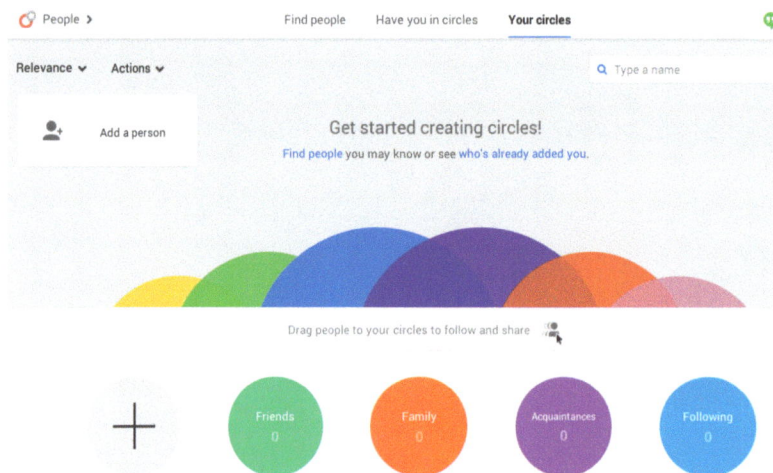

Figure 4.1: Your Circles page

Notice there are four pre-made Circles for your use. Google+ suggests the type of connection you may wish to put in each Circle:

- Friends – "Your real friends, the ones you feel comfortable sharing private details with."

- Family – "Your close and extended family, with as many or as few in-laws as you want."

- Acquaintances – "A good place to stick people you have met but are not particularly close to."

- Following – "People you do not know personally, but whose posts you find interesting."

These are merely suggestions, of course. You also see a Circle with a plus sign in it. This is used to create new, custom Circles. Let's begin by adding some contacts to the existing Circles. The add process is a necessary step in creating a custom Circle, so it's a good place to begin.

Adding People to Your Circle

There are two boxes in Figure 4.1: "Add a person" to the left and "Type a name" to the right. They do essentially the same thing, but differently. "Add a person" allows you to search for and add someone by their name or email address. The unique part of this feature is that you can add someone who's not yet on Google+. An email is sent to that person letting them know you added them to your Circles and also inviting them to join Google+. The "Type a name" feature only accepts names of people already on Google+.

You do not have to know the people you select for your Circles. For example, you could add Larry Page, Google's CEO, or Mark Zuckerberg, Facebook's CEO. You get to see their public updates in your stream (the information displayed on your Google+ homepage). However, your public updates only show in a special stream on their homepage called "Incoming." Unless, of course, they add you back, which they may or may not do as it's not mandatory. It should be noted that neither the names of your Circles ("Friends," "Family," etc.) are shared, nor who is in which Circle.

GOOGLE+ TIP

Lawyers should search for and add as many lawyers as possible to their Circles. Look for lawyers that are "popular" on Google+ and have many connections in various Circles. Be social and feel free to comment on, share, or recommend their posts.

Adding to Circles Using "Add a Person" Method

Let's add someone to your Friends Circle by email. Type in the email address of the person you wish to add (see Figure 4.2).

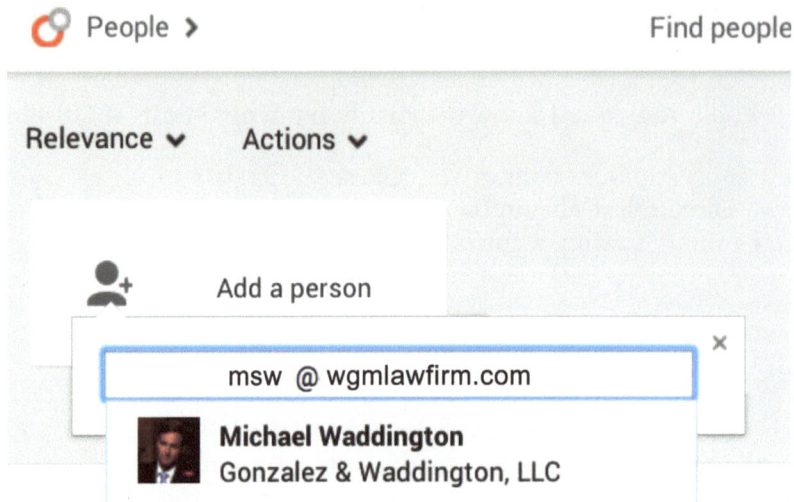

Figure 4.2: Adding a person by email

You'll see the email address you entered and the phrase "Add email@email.com by email" below the space in which you entered the address. The name is redacted in this example. If the address is correct, then hit "enter." This displays the following (see Figure 4.3):

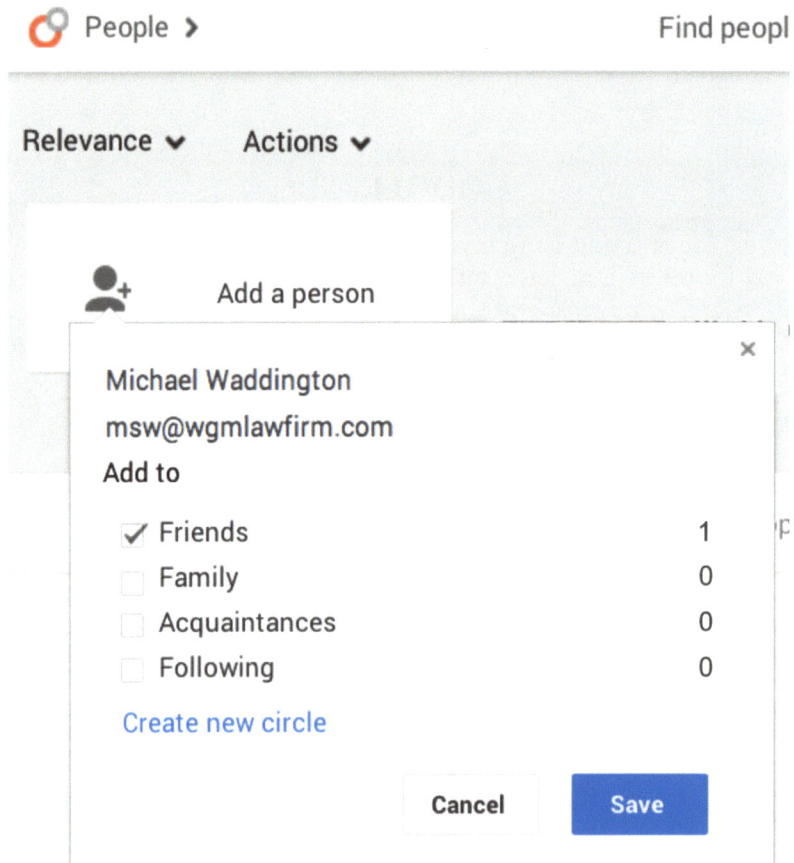

Figure 4.3: Assign person to Circle

Assigning a Person to Circle

You need to enter the person's name as you'd like it to appear. Remember, only you will see the name in your circle. Then, select the appropriate Circle, in this case, Friends. Then click "Save." If you click on the Friends Circle, you see that Michael Waddington was added (see Figure 4.4).

Editing Circle information

You can edit Circle information by clicking on the pencil in the Circle (see Figure 4.4). By clicking on the arrow, you can share the Circle with others on Google+. Lastly, you can delete the Circle by clicking on the trashcan.

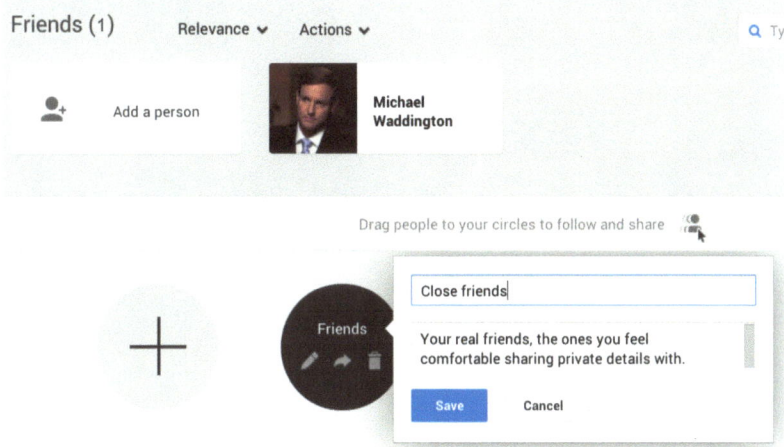

Figure 4.4: Editing Circle information

Adding to Circles Using "Type a Name" Method

Now we will add someone using the "Type a Name" function. Remember, this function searches and adds only those already on Google+. For example, type "Thomas Burnside" into the "Type a Name" box and hit "enter." You get the following screen. If you hover your cursor over the Thomas Burnside box you wish to add, a pop-up appears (see Figure 4.5).

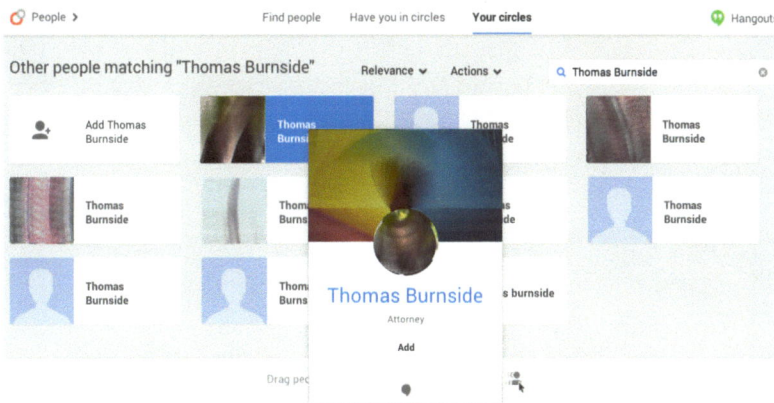

Figure 4.5: Adding by name only

There are two ways of adding Thomas to your Circles. One is clicking on "Add" at the bottom of the pop-up. The other is to drag the smaller icon with his name into the Circle of your choice, or the Circle with the plus sign if you want to add him to a new Circle. We will show you both ways, as they are slightly different.

Hover over the "Add" button at the bottom of the pop-up. A new box pops up (see Figure 4.6). Click "Create new circle" at the bottom of that pop-up; another pop-up appears asking you to name the new Circle. In this example, we will name it "Lawyers" (see Figure 4.7).

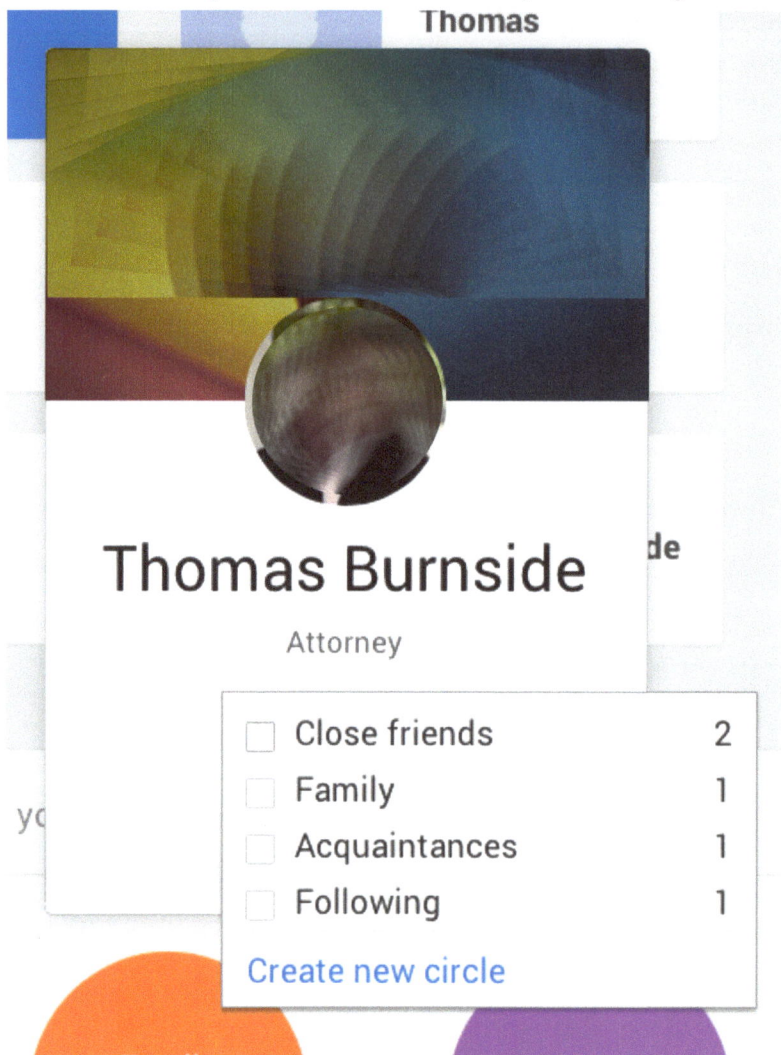

Figure 4.6: Create new Circle, method 1

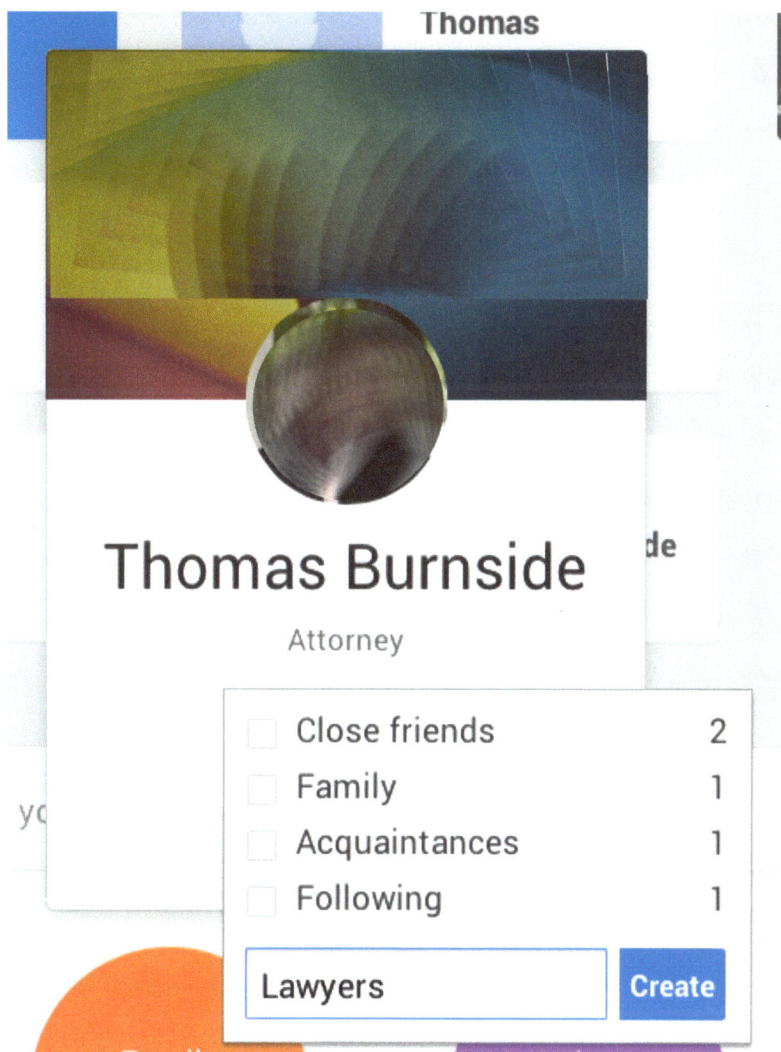

Figure 4.7: Name new Circle

The end result is a new Circle called "Lawyers" with Thomas Burnside as its initial member (see Figure 4.8).

Figure 4.8: New Circle

Creating a Circle Using the "Drag and Drop" Method

We will now create a new Circle using the "drag and drop" method. The process for finding people is the same as our Thomas Burnside example above. Only this time, we will use Abraham Lincoln. Type "Abraham Lincoln" into the search box. You'll see the results below (see Figure 4.9).

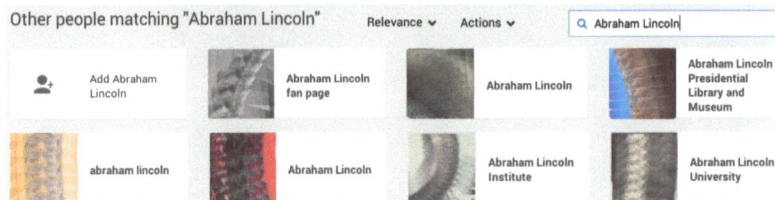

Figure 4.9: Abraham Lincoln search results

Select Abraham Lincoln University's icon with the hand tool that appears when you hover your cursor over the icon. Do this by holding down the left mouse button. Then, drag and drop the icon into the Circle with the plus sign (see Figure 4.10).

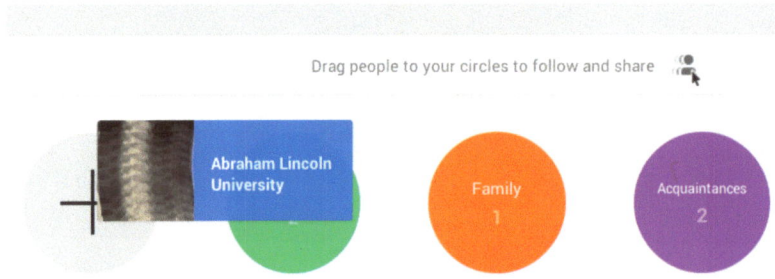

Figure 4.10: Drag and drop add

You now have the option of clearing the new, as yet unnamed Circle, or naming it (see Figure 4.11).

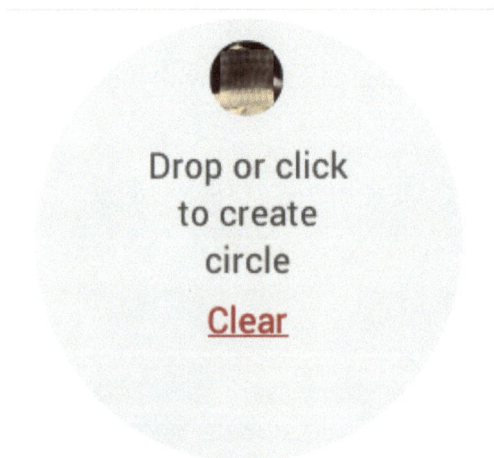

Figure 4.11: Clear or name Circle

Since we want to create the new Circle, click on the "click to create circle" text or drop the icon in the circle. This is the screen that results (see Figure 4.12). Then, name the circle (i.e. American Heroes).

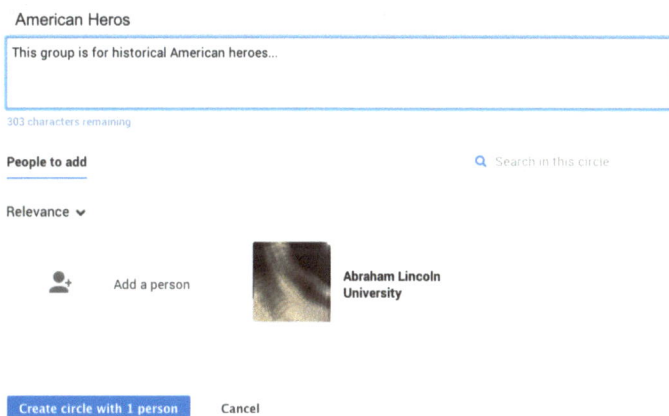

Figure 4.12: Name and create new Circle

Once you name the Circle and give it a description (optional), click "Create circle with 1 person." The results are below (see Figure 4.13):

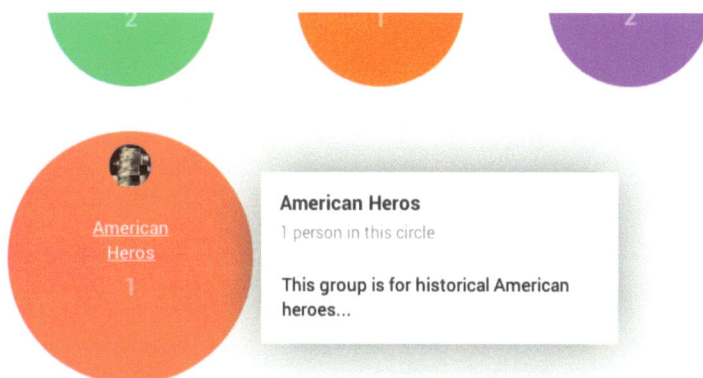

Figure 4.13: Another new Circle

Every time you post, you get to choose which Circle sees that post. This becomes very important when we get into maximizing Google+ for your practice.

Who Can See Your Posts?

When you post information on Google+, you have the following options:

- A single individual - Type the person's name or email address; this post is the equivalent of a private message.

- A specific Circle – Posts are viewable to every member of that Circle.

- A group of Circles - Any combination of your Circles.

- Your Circles - All of your Circles.

- Extended Circles – All of your Circles and everyone in all of their Circles sees the post.

- Public – The post is viewable by everyone on the Internet, just like a tweet is visible to everyone on Twitter.

If you want to keep up on what's going on in your Circles (and you do, more on that in the next chapter), then you can do it from your Google+ homepage (see Figure 4.14). You have the choice of reading posts from your Circles, Friends, Acquaintances, Following, or More. Under More, you'll see the two Circles not visible on the main navigation bar.

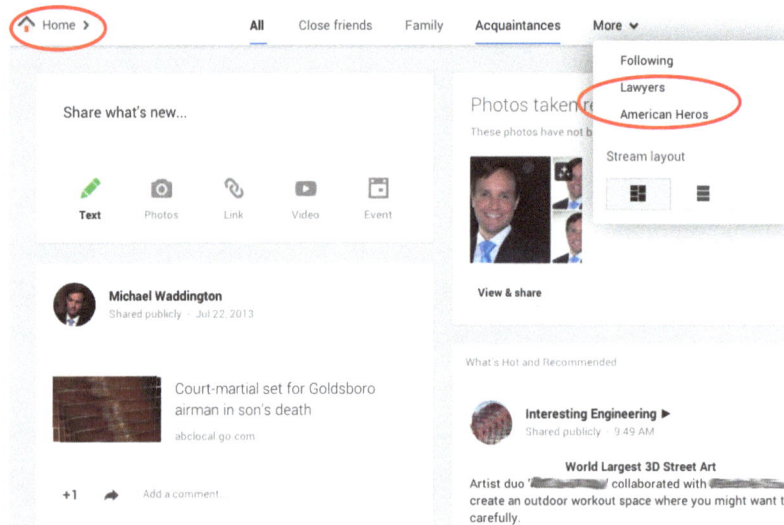

Figure 4.14: Read posts made by those in your Circles

That does it for setting up, managing, and monitoring your Circles. You now have the tools necessary to use Google+. The next two chapters will show you how to use it to grow your practice.

Chapter 5: Marketing Your Practice on Google+

Your personal profile and Circles are set up. Now, it's time to set up the pages you need to market your practice on Google+. Google+ provides two distinct pages – Google+ for Business and Google+ Local (also known as Google Places) to get the job done. This process can be confusing, so seek expert assistance if necessary.

Setting Up Your Google+ for Business Page

The first thing you are going to do is set up your Google+ for Business Page. Click on "Pages" at the left of your screen (see Figure 5.1).

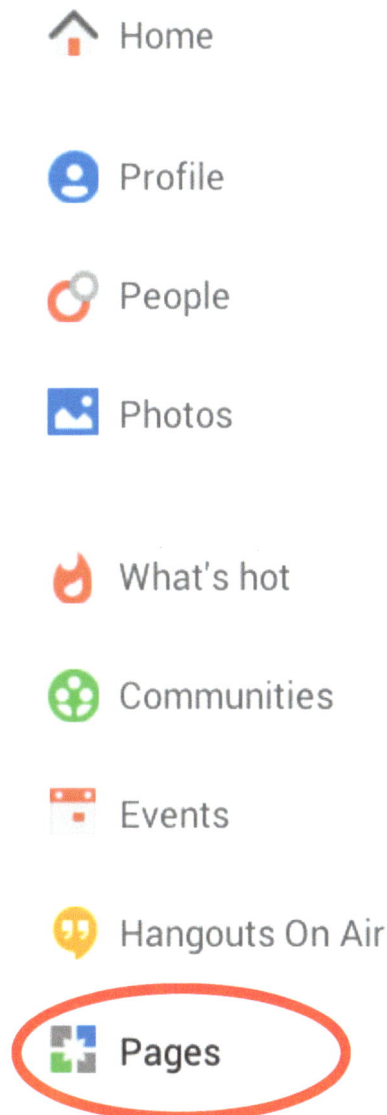

Figure 5.1: Finding the Page button

This takes you to the following screen (see Figure 5.2):

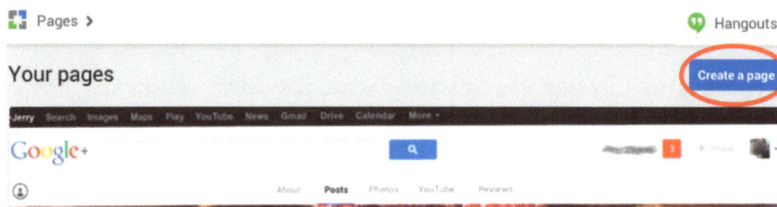

Figure 5.2: Create a Page screen

Click on "Create a page" at the upper right of your screen. This takes you to the next screen (see Figure 5.3):

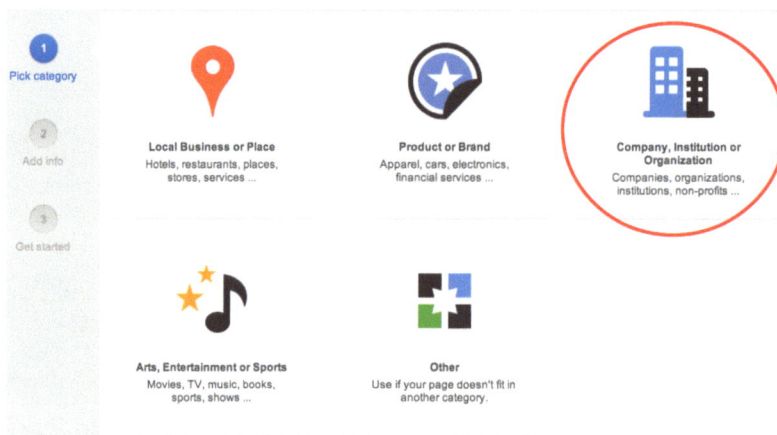

Figure 5.3: Step two of setting up business page

Since you are setting up your Google+ for Business page first, ignore the "Local Business or Place" option for now. Click on the "Company, Institution or Organization" option. This takes you to the following page, where you'll select "Legal" from the drop-down menu of organization types (see Figure 5.4).

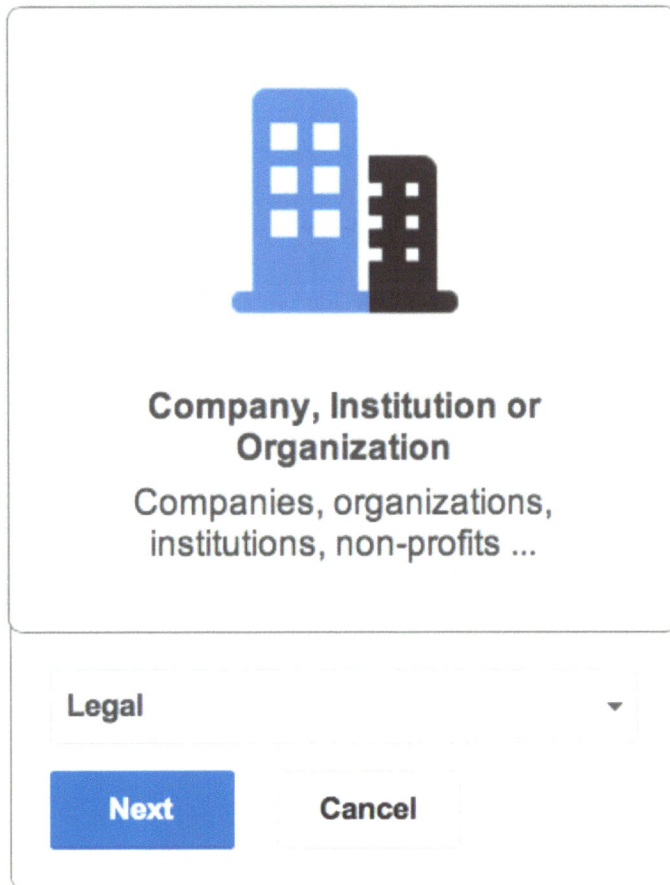

Figure 5.4: Select category of business from the drop down menu

Click "Next" to get to the following page (see Figure 5.5):

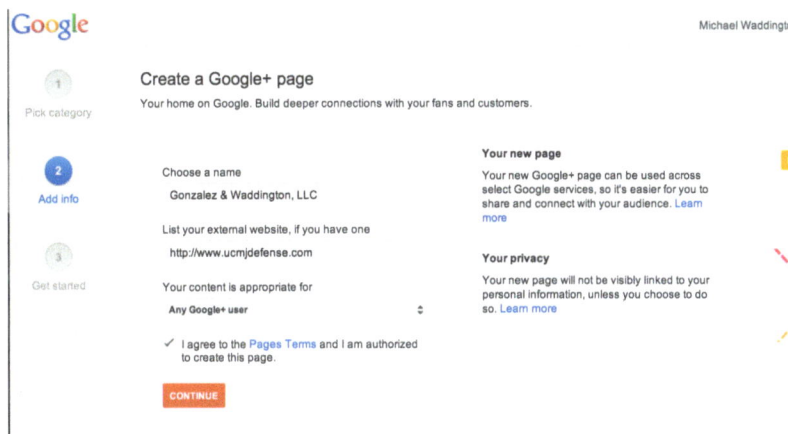

Figure 5.5: Naming your Google+ Business Page

Enter your official business name. This makes you more easily identifiable on Google+. You should also enter your firm's website if you have one. Google+ requires that you select an option from the "Your content is appropriate for" drop-down menu. The choices are:

- Any Google+ user

- Users 18 and older

- Users 21 and older

- Alcohol related

These selections are meant to prevent participation of those under the appropriate age. Since you are not selling alcohol, you do not need to select "Alcohol related." Interestingly, no matter what option you choose, underage users can view your content, but they cannot participate in discussions or make posts or comments on your Page. Since the goal of your practice Page is to reach as many potential clients as possible, we suggest choosing the "Any Google+ user" option.

Check the box agreeing to the Pages Terms and click "continue." Your Page appears (see Figure 5.6):

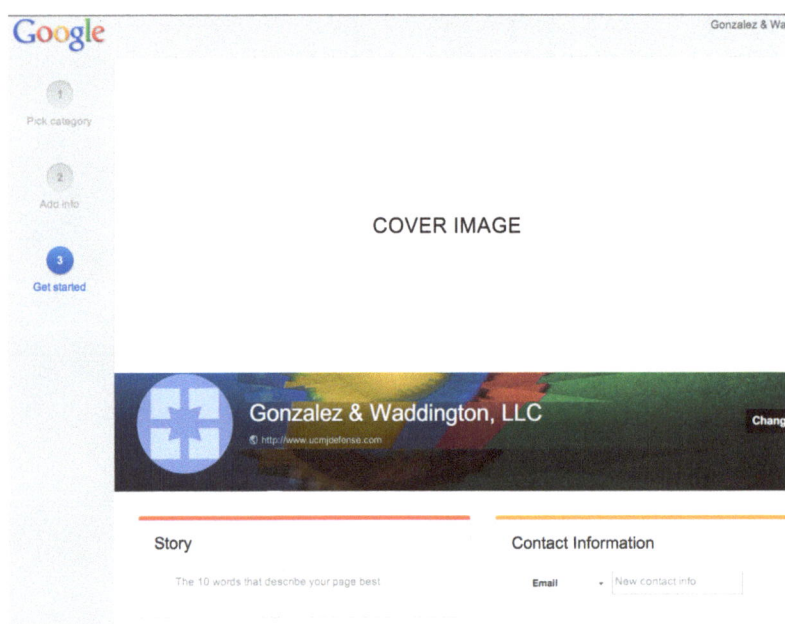

Figure 5.6: Initial appearance of your practice Page

Now it's time to customize your Page. Fill in the information requested at the bottom of the page (see Figure 5.7).

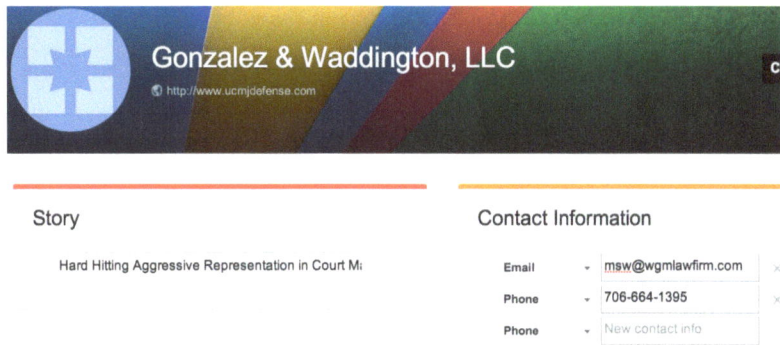

Figure 5.7: Customize Page, step 1

The page should look familiar (see Figure 5.8):

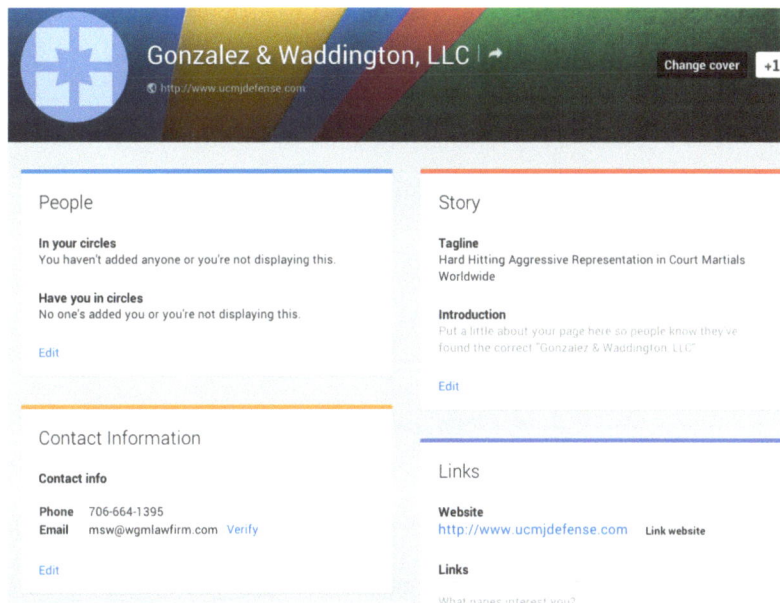

Figure 5.8: About section of practice Page

It looks familiar because you have seen it (and completed it) for your personal Page. One thing to note: At this point, you are working in your new business Page. However, should you want to go to your personal Page, just click on the square at the upper right of the page.

When you click on the square button, you see the following (see Figure 5.9):

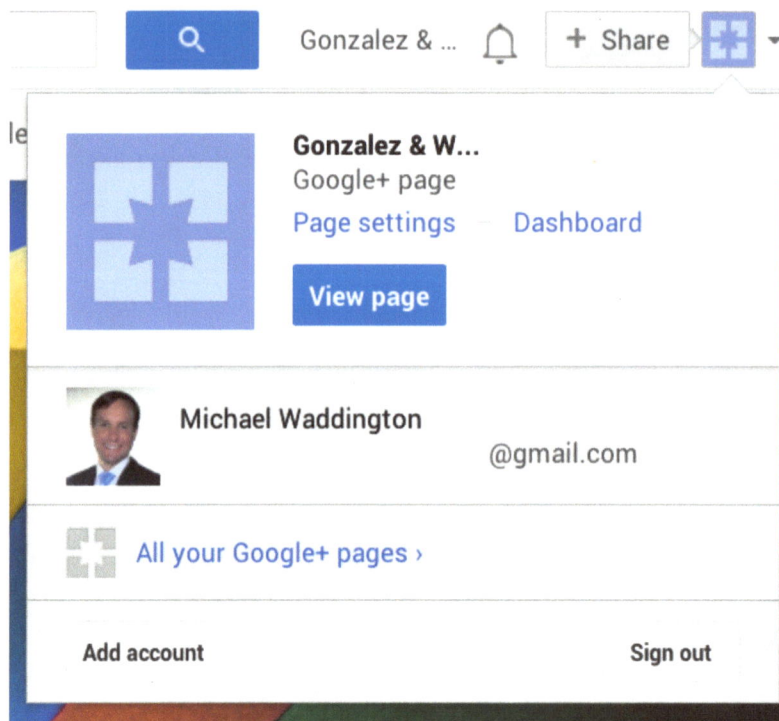

Figure 5.9: Choice of Page to view

At this point, you can select your personal Page or any other Google+ pages you may have; you may also set your page settings (as you did with your personal Page), or modify your Page managers. You, as the owner, are automatically a manager. You can add others in your practice as managers, enabling them to post, edit Circles, and adjust Page settings. For now, let's assume you are the only manager. As for the Page settings, we suggest the same settings used with your personal Page.

On your business Page, there are four sections you can modify: People, Story, Contact Information, and Links. This process is exactly the same as it was with your personal Page. You can refer back to earlier sections if you need a refresher. Likewise, you will change the cover and add a photo to your practice Page using the same methods as your personal Page.

Your practice Page has four pre-set Circles: Customers, Following, Team Members, and VIPs. As with your personal Circles, Google+ suggests the type of connection you may want to put in each:

- Customers – "All the people or organizations you want to build deeper relationships with."

- Following – "People you do not know personally, but whose posts you find interesting."

- Team members – "The people you will share the inside scoop with."

- VIPs – "Your most loyal customers and closest partners."

We will set up your practice Page's Circles shortly. For now, you should select the settings for viewing these Circles. Even though no one sees the names of the Circles you have, Customers (which we will later rename Clients) should be made non-viewable by others. They may not be identifiable, but some Clients prefer the anonymity. In keeping with this line of thought, we also suggest that VIPs not be used for clients, as Google+ suggests, but rather for important partners,, unless you choose to make that Circle non-viewable too. Click "Save" when you are done.

As before, click on the People menu at the left side of the screen to get to the page where we will set up your Circles (see Figure 5.10).

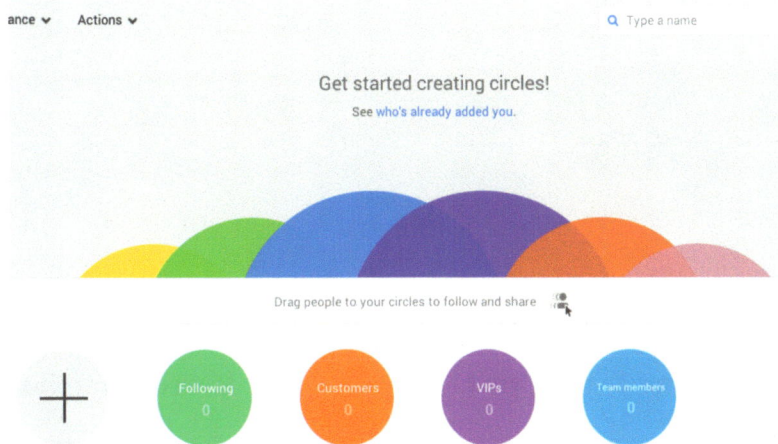

Figure 5.10: Setting up your practice Circles

There is another difference between this and your personal Circles: The "Add a person by email" option is gone. You can only add to these Circles using the "Type a name" option. Before you start adding people, you should organize the Circles in a way that will better serve a law practice. Click inside the Customers Circle; this opens it for editing as seen below (see Figure 5.11):

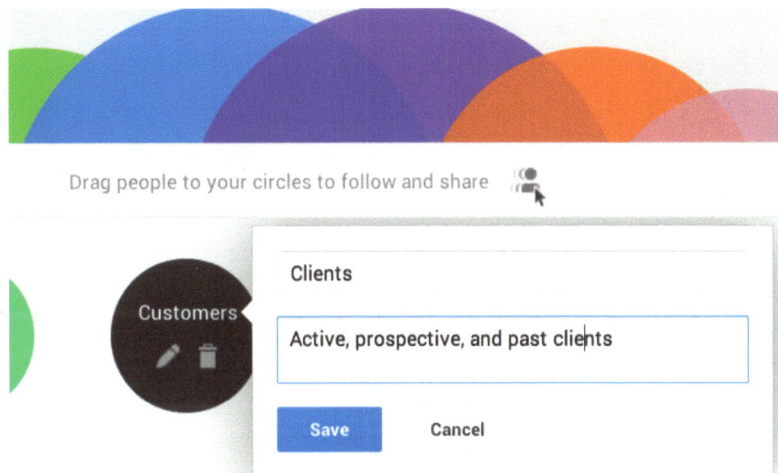

Figure 5.11: Editing the Customers Circle

One item of note is that the share arrow is gone. You can edit or delete these Circles, but can not share them. Click on the pencil to begin the edits. Click "Save" when you are done (see Figure 5.12).

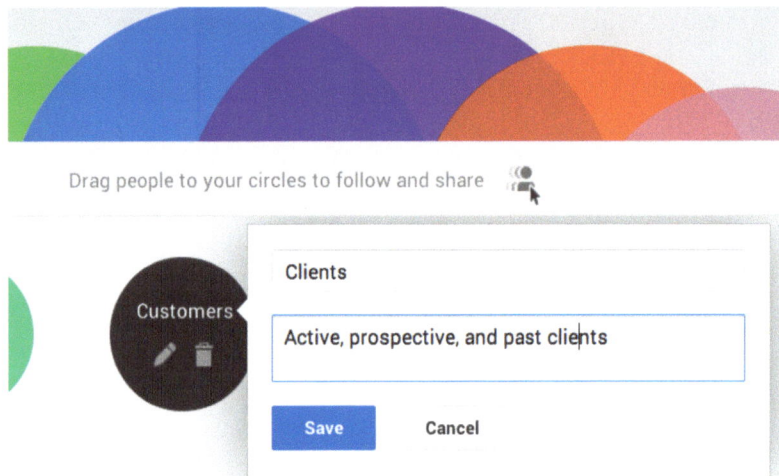

Figure 5.12: Customers become Clients

Also, you should rename "Team Members" to "Fellow Lawyers" for use as a professional networking Circle (see Figure 5.13):

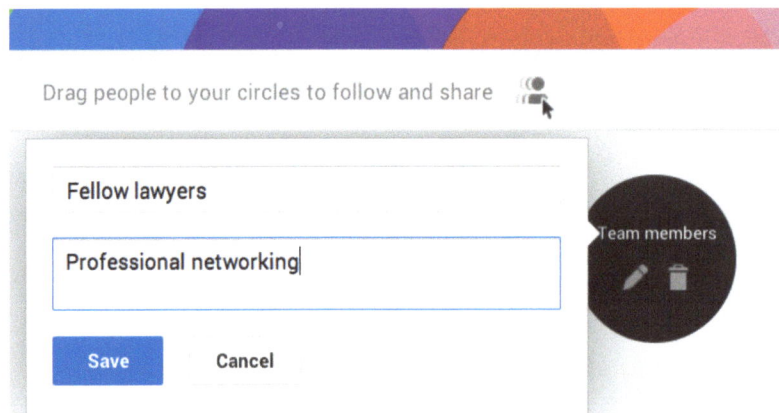

Figure 5.13: Team Members become Fellow Lawyers

Of course, you are free to customize the Circles as you see fit; delete those you do not want and add new ones using the Circle with the plus sign. Adding people to your practice Circles is done the same way as with your personal Circles, so we will not duplicate it here. Congratulations, you have completed setting up your practice Page! Next, you will set up your Google+ Local Page.

Setting Up Your Google+ Local Page

Go back to Pages and click "Create a page" (see Figure 5.14).

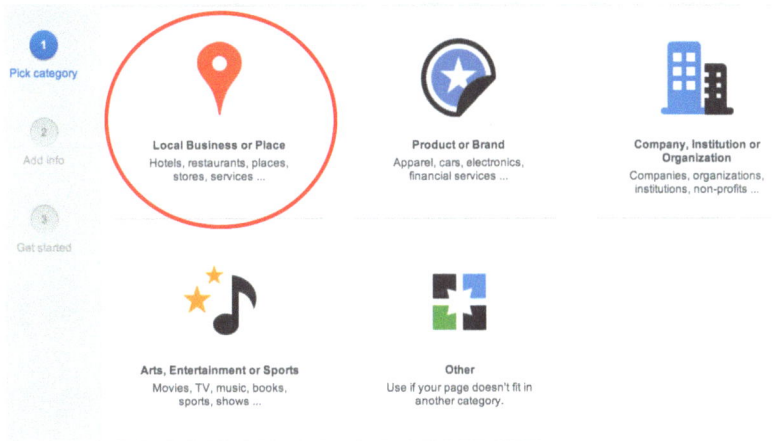

Figure 5.14: Create a page screen

This time, click on the "Local Business or Place" option. This takes you to the following screen (see Figure 5.15):

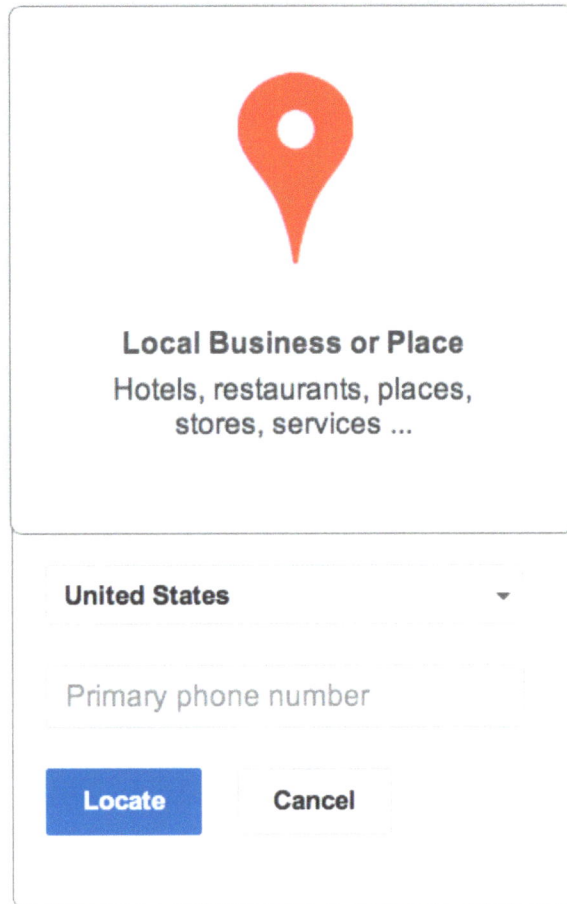

Figure 5.15: Step 1 of setting up a Local Page

Google+ locates your business by your official business telephone number. Enter it and hit "Locate." The following results appear (see Figure 5.16):

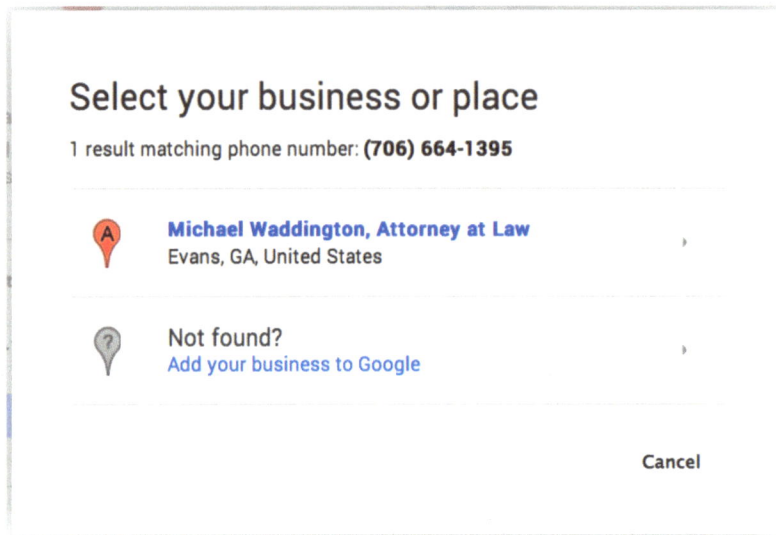

Select your business or place

1 result matching phone number: **(706) 664-1395**

A **Michael Waddington, Attorney at Law**
Evans, GA, United States ›

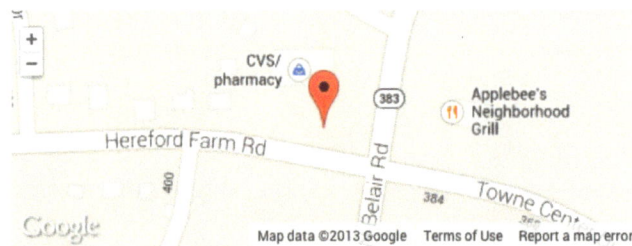

? Not found? ›
Add your business to Google

Cancel

Figure 5.16: Locate business by phone

Your options are clicking on the located business if it's yours or adding your business to Google. Let's click on the business located. Later, we will cover how to add your practice to Google. After clicking on the business located, you get the following page (see Figure 5.17):

Confirm your info

Phone
(706) 664-1395

Business name and address
Michael Waddington, Attorney at Law

Evans, GA, United States

Map data ©2013 Google   Terms of Use   Report a map error
Location not quite right? Drag the marker to the correct spot.
Category
Attorney

Cancel   OK

Figure 5.17: Confirm your business

If everything is correct, click "OK." Google+ then asks you to position the pin on the map if it is not positioned correctly. Do this by dragging the pin. The next screen asks for basic information about your practice (see Figure 5.18). This is exactly the same process used for your Google+ Business Page; repeat that process with the same information.

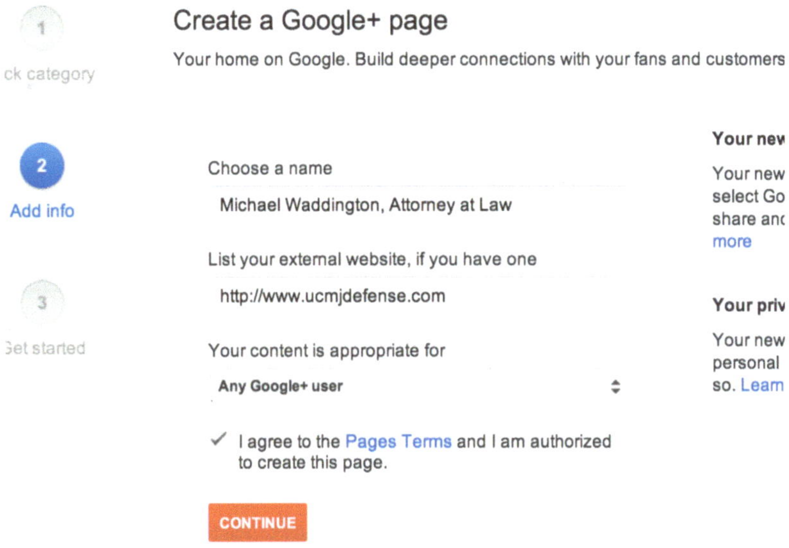

Figure 5.18: Enter practice–specific information

The next page you'll see is your Google+ Local Page (see Figure 5.19):

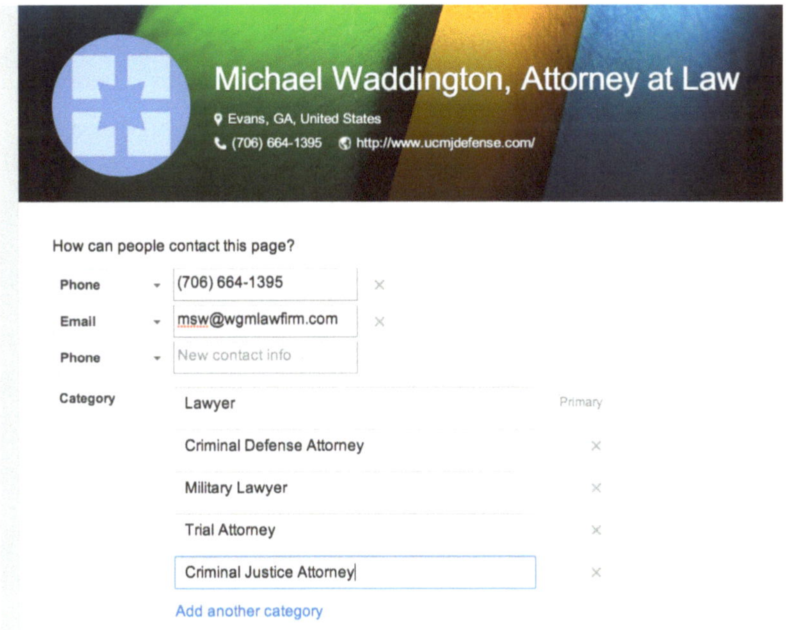

Figure 5.19: First view of Local Page

Click on "Finish" when you have completed the information. This takes you to the following page (see Figure 5.20):

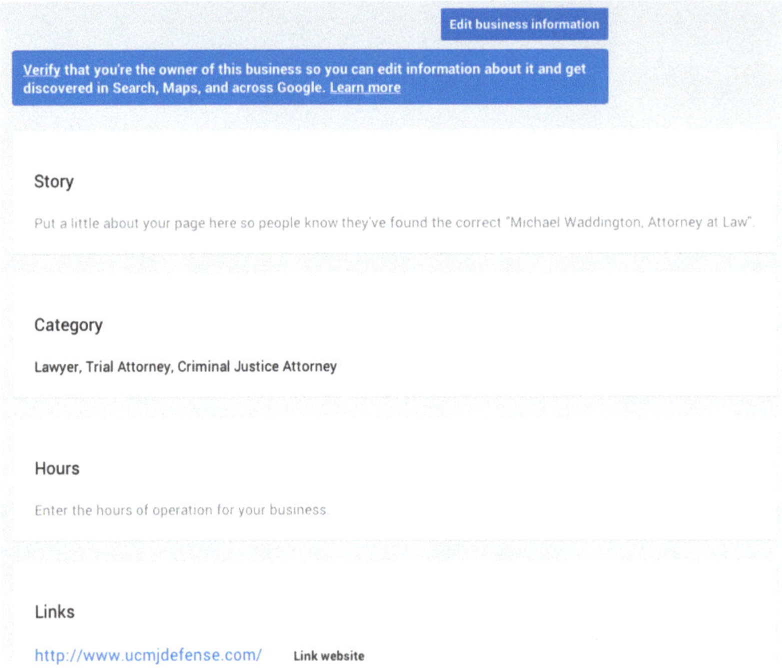

Figure 5.20: Information and verification page

Here, you can add practice-specific information by filling out each section. There is a "Verify" bar near the top of the page. Since your page is new, Google will send a postcard to your physical address in order to verify your ownership of the page. The postcard will be sent to your business address and has a five-digit PIN that you need to enter to complete the verification process. It usually arrives within two weeks after you start the verification process. Once you have been verified, any time you change information on this page, Google will reverify you as the business owner. Typically, the reverification is done by a telephone call to your business number.

According to Google, "It can take up to two weeks after you have verified (by phone or postcard) for the changes to appear live in Google+ Local. So do not delay — all in all, you have a 2-4 week lag time between creating your page and getting it on Google+ Local. Now is your time to claim your place, and take advantage of Google+ Local."

A great benefit of the Google+ Local Page is the return in SERPs (search engine results pages) when a potential client searches for lawyers in your city (see Figure 5.21).

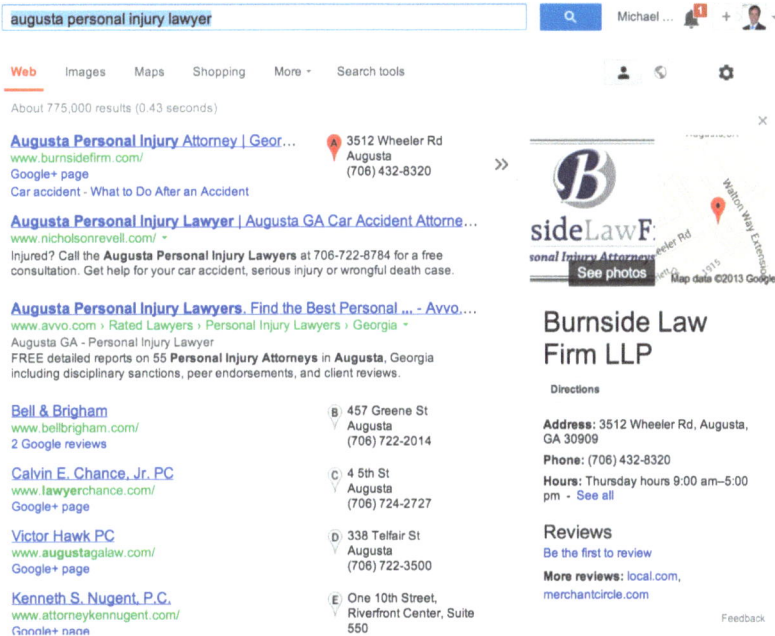

Figure 5.21: Example of benefit of Local Page

The SERP returned for "Augusta personal injury lawyer" on Google shows several results. However, if you hover over Burnside Law Firm, LLC, its Local Page pops up on the right of the screen.

Linking Your Website to Your Google+ Business Page

You can link your website to your Google+ Business Page (not the Local Page) by clicking on "Link website" from the About page of your Google+ Business Page (see Figures 5.22 & 5.23).

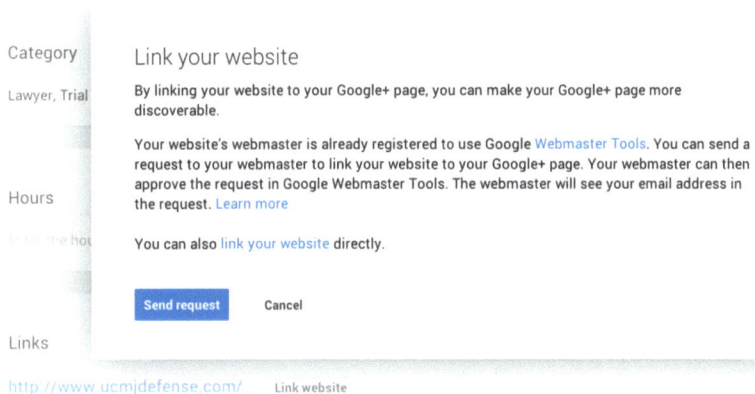

Figure 5.22: Linking your practice website to your Google+ Business Page

Category

Lawyer, Trial

Link your website

By adding a short line of code to **http://www.ucmjdefense.com/**, you can make your Google+ page eligible to show up on the right hand side of the Google search page for relevant queries and make your Google+ page more discoverable. Learn more

Hours

Enter the hou

Ask your site's webmaster to add the following line of code to your site's homepage:

```
<a href="https://plus.google.com/102862938931390134379" rel="publisher">Google+</a>
```

You can also email these instructions to your webmaster

Test website   Cancel

Links

http://www.ucmjdefense.com/   Link website

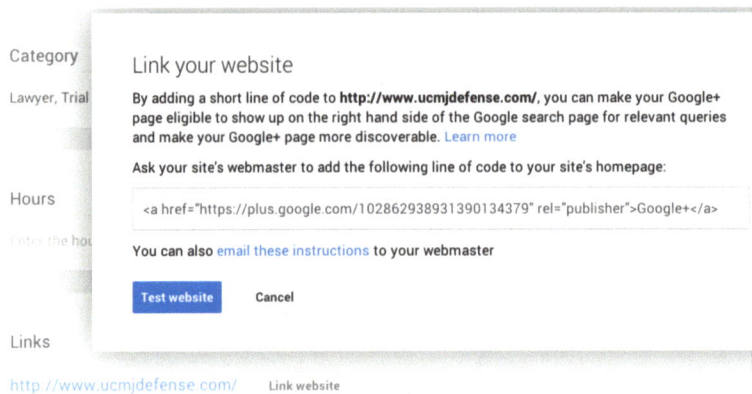

Figure 5.23: Direct linking to your website by inserting code

Chapter 6: Develop a Google+ Strategy to Grow Your Legal Network

Now you have everything set up. In this chapter, we will focus on specific actions you can take to grow your practice using Google+. Some of these involve creating posts, sharing interesting items, following (and being followed in return), creating events, chats, communities, and much more.

Managing Your Stream

Your Stream is found by clicking "Home" on the left side menu. The Stream is where you see posts from those in your Circles, those you are following, those who follow you, as well as your own posts (see Figure 6.1).

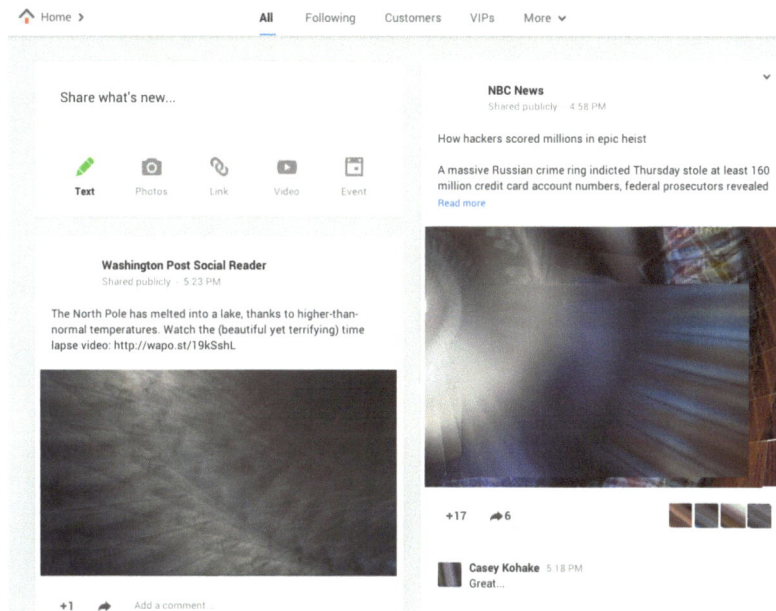

Figure 6.1: Snapshot of a Stream

The Stream view (shown at the top of Figure 6.1) allows you to choose what content you see. This snapshot shows "All," the option bolded above. You can see the options mirror the names of your Circles; "More" allows you to choose Circles that aren't shown in the choices above.

Even though Google+ is a tool used to promote your practice, it is still, at heart, a social networking site. This means that you, the lawyer, need to be actively social in your promotion. The more active you are on Google+, the greater the opportunity to expand your network and your practice. We realize you are busy, but even 30 minutes a day can help increase your business. Many lawyers go online over the weekend. Taking the time to make a few interesting posts on Saturday or Sunday is a great way to connect, as people are more active on social networks on weekends.

Managing a Google+ presence does not require hours a day. After you make some initial connections by inviting clients, fellow lawyers and finding those already on Google+, your Stream will become more active. Of course, as you post items yourself, you initiate even more activity.

Text Posts with Links

If you are a criminal defense attorney and you find an interesting news story on the Internet, post it on Google+. Copy the website address (the URL) and go to your Stream. At the top of your Stream, you see a box with the text "Share what's new..." (see Figure 6.2).

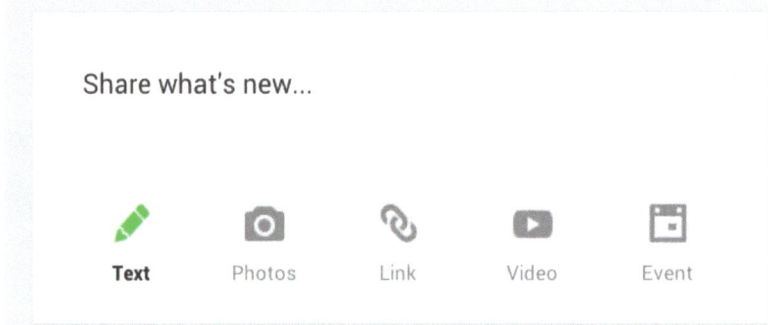

Figure 6.2: Share what's new... by posting

Click in the box. You'll see this view (see Figure 6.3):

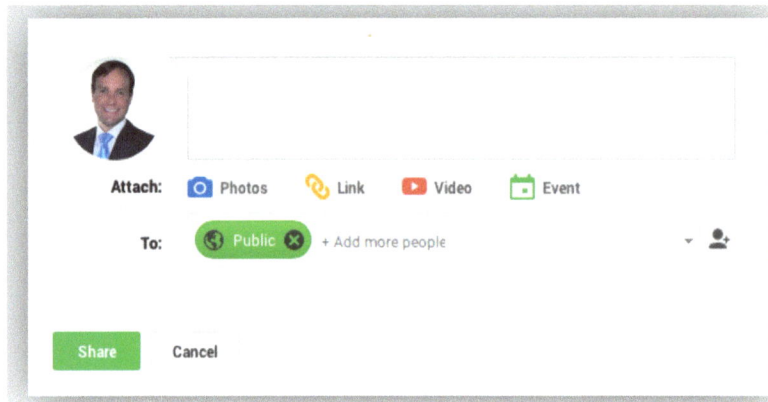

Figure 6.3: Posting box

Posting Links

Copy the URL (website address) of the site you want to post, in this case, a link from the Time website (http://nation.time.com/2013/07/23/why-general-sinclairs-lawyer-wants-the-chain-of-command-delinked/). Click on the "Link" option in the posting box and paste the link (see Figure 6.4).

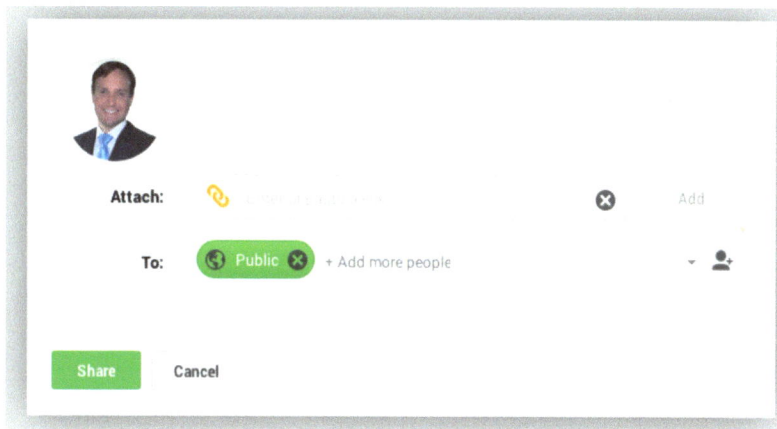

Figure 6.4: Enter or paste link

Google+ inserts the link into your post (see Figure 6.5).

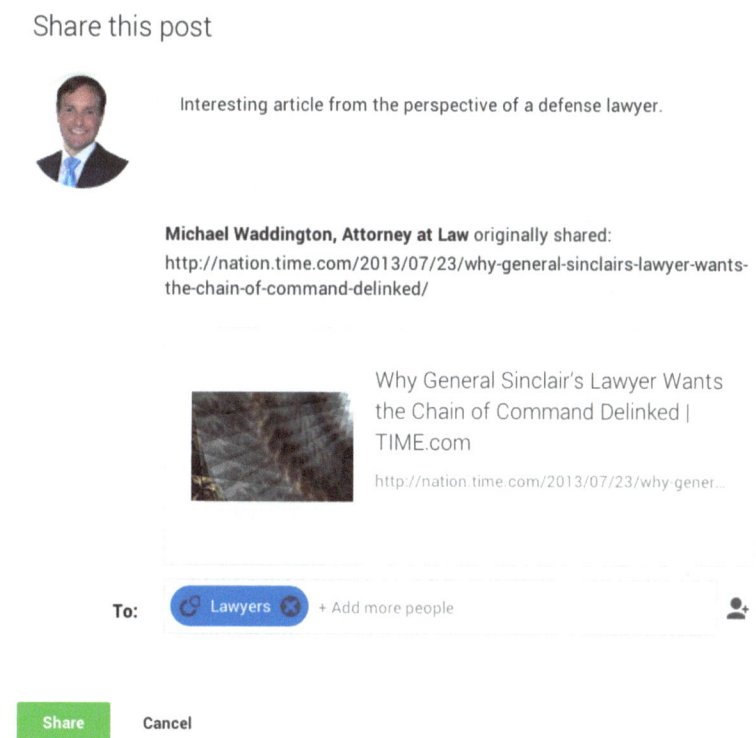

Figure 6.5: Link inserted in post

Now it's your time to shine. Write a brief summary or commentary about what caught your attention on the linked site. Choose who gets to view the post. In this case, Public is the best choice. Then click "Send." This post is now visible on your Stream.

Posting is not just telling others about sites you find interesting. This is your opportunity to market yourself. For example, you can link to items on your own site using the same method. Or, take a topic from your specialty and write an article on it to draw in potential clients.

Posts with Photographs

There are other ways that updates benefit your practice. If you are a personal injury attorney, for instance, you could write an article highlighting accidents caused by faulty traffic lights and how your practice helps injured drivers gain compensation. Then, add a photo to drive the point home. In this case, a public domain photo. Click in the "Share what's new…" box, as before. Write the text and then click on the "Photos" option. The following box opens (see Figure 6.6):

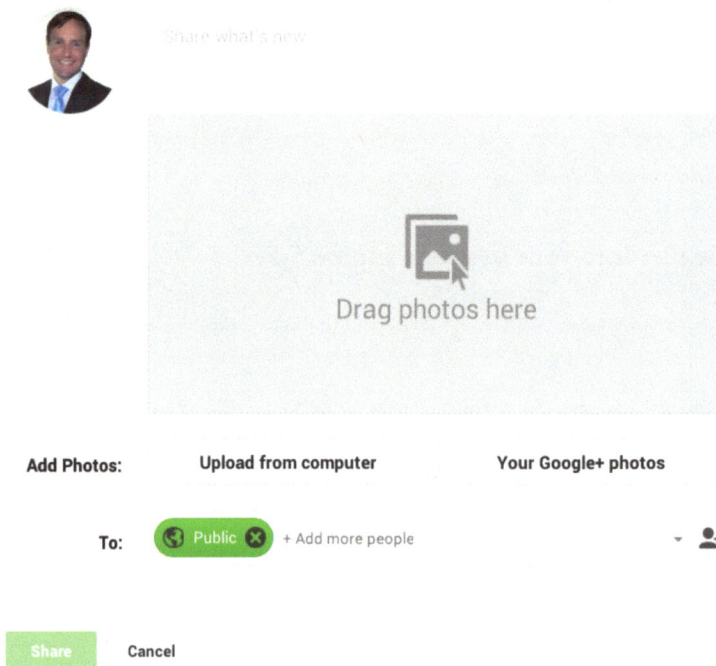

Figure 6.6: Add photo to post

Using the options offered (as we did during your profile set-up) upload the photo. Select who gets to view the post, in this case "Clients" to attract clients and then click "Share." This post now appears in your Stream. We're not done yet, though. You can also upload videos to the Stream.

Video Posts

Uploading a video requires that you have a video, of course. If you are using YouTube to broadcast your own videos, Google+ allows you to upload these; if you use a video camera, you can save the video files to your computer and upload them as you did photos. Google+ even has an option for recording videos if your computer has a webcam and microphone.

GOOGLE+ TIP

Every time you post a new video to YouTube or your website, you should share it on your Google+ page. This helps get your video extra exposure and may help your video rank higher in the search engines

Recording Videos with Google+

Check that you have allowed Google+ to access your camera and microphone. If you also select "Remember," you will not have to repeat this step next time. Then click "Close." Your camera and microphone are now active. Simply click on "Record" to begin. You have up to 15 minutes of recording space per video. Once you are finished, click "Recording" to stop and "Add video" to upload it.

Tips for making a high-quality video:

1. Plan out your script – your message – before you begin. Adlibbing only creates excessive pauses and "ums," which do not sound professional.

2. Make sure your backdrop is suitable. You do not want prospective clients looking past you at what's happening outside your office window.

3. Do a test video first. You can delete it and start over by clicking "Start over" in the bottom right of the screen. The test video allows you to ensure your voice is being recorded properly and that you are speaking at the correct volume.

4. Stay on topic (follow your script). Tangents may confuse prospective clients.

5. Keep the video informative and end it with a call to action. You are passing on information to prospective clients; now you want them to call you to act on the information.

Host a Webinar

Google+ webinars are a great way to educate and attract new clients, as well as keep current clients abreast of new developments in the law. One great benefit of doing a Google+ webinar is that it is free. Webinars are particularly effective for practices such as estate planning or tax law, which involve ongoing client relationships. As laws – and other regulations, such as Medicare – change, their impact on your current clients may require them to update their own planning. By informing them of the changes, rather than letting them be surprised, you are strengthening relationships, saving your clients possible trouble, and getting repeat business.

If fifteen minutes is not long enough to adequately cover the topic, then make it a series. A series will give you time to cover the topic and keep clients – current and prospective – coming back. Those who can't wait until the next installment will call you for an appointment. These methods are active means of posting original information, whether it is your articles and videos or your insightful commentary on other peoples' information. All of these showcase your talent and skill as an attorney in your field. In fact, as THE attorney viewers should be calling.

Commenting on Posts

Original posts are not the only way you can market yourself on Google+. Commenting on others' posts is also a way to build up your practice. Networking with other attorneys, mentioned several times already, is also good for business. As you build relationships, you build a knowledge base to support you when you have questions, as well as a potential referral network. Commenting is very easy (see Figure 6.7).

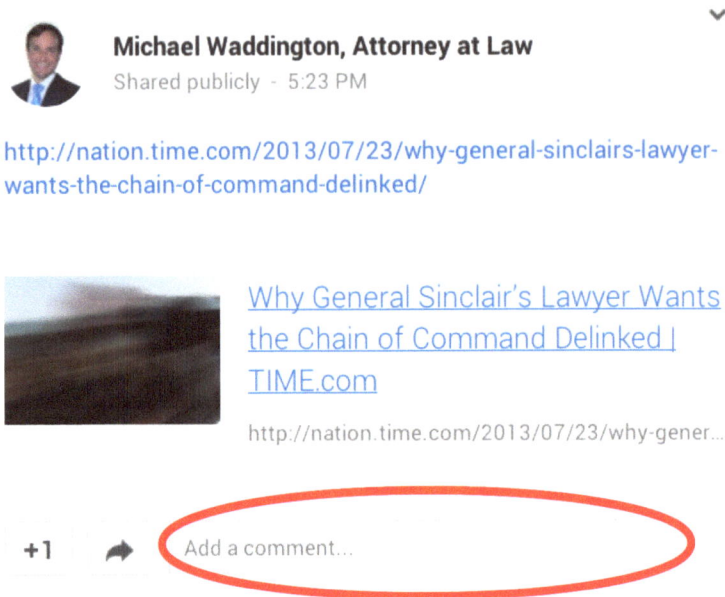

Figure 6.7: Adding a comment to a post

GOOGLE+ TIP

Make sure your comments are relevant. Unrelated comments will be considered spam and will not make you any friends.

+1's

Next, let's look at the "+1's," Google+'s version of Facebook's "Likes." If you see a post you agree with or simply like, but do not have anything to add in a comment, click on the "+1" at the bottom left of the post (see Figure 6.8).

Michael Waddington, Attorney at Law
Shared publicly · 5:23 PM

http://nation.time.com/2013/07/23/why-general-sinclairs-lawyer-wants-the-chain-of-command-delinked/

Why General Sinclair's Lawyer Wants the Chain of Command Delinked | TIME.com

http://nation.time.com/2013/07/23/why-gener...

+1   Add a comment...

Figure 6.8: The ubiquitous Google+ +1

Google offers a great explanation of the +1's meaning on its support page, About the +1 Button:

"+1 is how you signal your appreciation for anything that grabs your attention on Google+ or on your favorite websites. When you read a post that makes you want to cheer, +1 is your applause; when you watch a video that has you in stitches, +1 is your laughter; when you see a photo that perfectly captures that special moment, +1 is your 5-star review.

+1's on Google+

When you +1 a post on Google+, the creator of that post and the people the post was shared with can see your +1. The creator of the post will receive a notification that you +1'd their post.

To remove your +1, just click the +1 button again.

+1's Outside of Google+

When you +1 something on a website, your +1 will be added to the total number of +1's shown in the count. When someone who has you in his or her Circles views content that you have +1'd, your +1 may be highlighted next to the +1 count.

+1's are public, so only +1 pages when you are comfortable sharing your recommendation with the world. Once you have +1'd something on the web, you can then share the content with your Circles on Google+.

Another use for +1s is profile recommendation. You go to the profiles of those you follow, those who follow you, and those in your Circles and +1 them. In turn, they can +1 you back. These +1 recommendations let viewers know that you are well thought of by others. You should also give your own profile a +1. This is the equivalent of voting for yourself, which is permitted on Google+.

Following and Sharing

Simply put, it's a matter of semantics. On Google+, you are going to see these terms regularly. Google+ decided that "Follow" as a verb sounded much better than "Circle." When you add someone to your Circles (and vice versa), you are, in essence, following them.

Sharing is posting. Whenever you post something, you are sharing. There is one little twist, though. When you are reading others' posts, you see the "Share" button (with an arrow on it) at the bottom left of the post (see Figure 6.9). In this example, the "1" in the "Share" button indicates that one other person has already shared it.

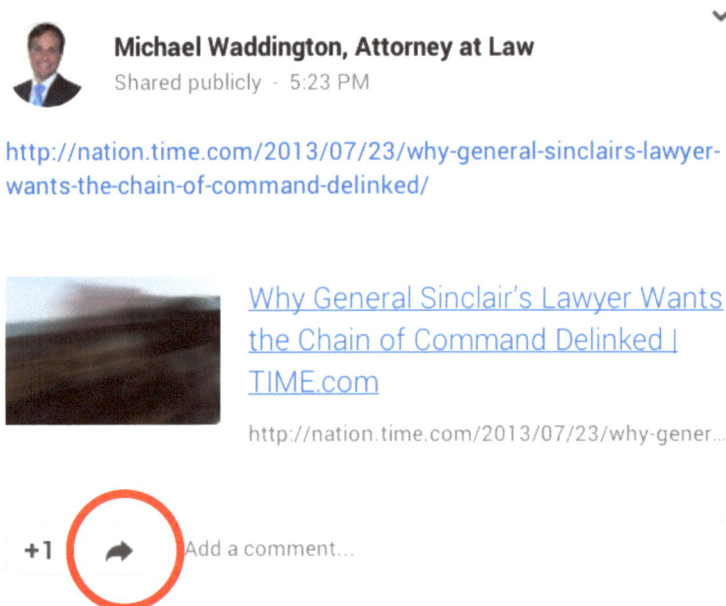

Michael Waddington, Attorney at Law
Shared publicly · 5:23 PM

http://nation.time.com/2013/07/23/why-general-sinclairs-lawyer-wants-the-chain-of-command-delinked/

Why General Sinclair's Lawyer Wants the Chain of Command Delinked | TIME.com

http://nation.time.com/2013/07/23/why-gener...

+1   Add a comment...

Figure 6.9: The Share button

If you click on the button, you can share the original post and the post's share history with your own Circles (see Figure 6.10). Adding your own comment to the share makes it more valuable to the people who see it, in this case, your Clients Circle.

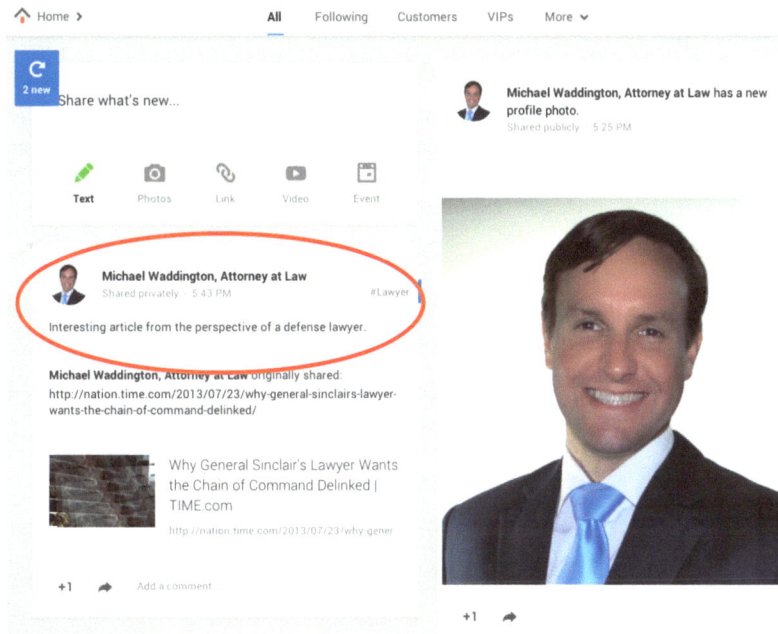

Figure 6.10: A shared post

Monitoring Your Circles

We've covered the importance of Circles already. We've also covered the importance of keeping a current presence on Google+. The two come together in that you must monitor and interact with your Circles to get value from them.

We suggest spending at least 15-20 minutes a day reading your Stream. This is where you will see what's going on with your Circles. 30 minutes is even better, maybe with a cup of coffee in the morning or a glass of wine in the evening while you relax. While your time is precious, the benefits of 15-30 minutes a day spent on Google+ are too good to ignore. If you prefer, you can limit your viewing to certain Circles. Rather than read about happenings in your friends' and families' lives – which you may decide to save for the weekend – limit your time to your Client Circle or your Team Members Circle.

This is easy to do. When you are viewing your Stream, look at the top of the page. As we mentioned earlier in the chapter, the underlined option is the current view. Just click on any of the selections to change to that view.

Another easy way of keeping up is to view one Circle per day and rotate them. You have set your notifications so you will not miss a comment or a question on anything you have posted. So if it's urgent, you will know. You may set aside time in your calendar for Google+ so that one hour a week is devoted to nothing more than marketing – creating webinars, articles, etc. You should comment and post at least once daily, though, to keep your presence fresh.

The Power of Hangouts

Google+ Hangouts is a powerful way to connect with your clients and potential clients. Hangouts can also help you become a respected authority in your legal field, which can lead to clients and referrals. Hangouts are video chats that you schedule with one of your Circles and other invited guests. This service is free and does not require expensive equipment or rentals. Even better, it is easy to set up and record.

Setting Up a Hangout

Hangouts can be set up in a couple different ways. First, click on Hangouts On Air, in the left navigation column (see Figure 6.11).

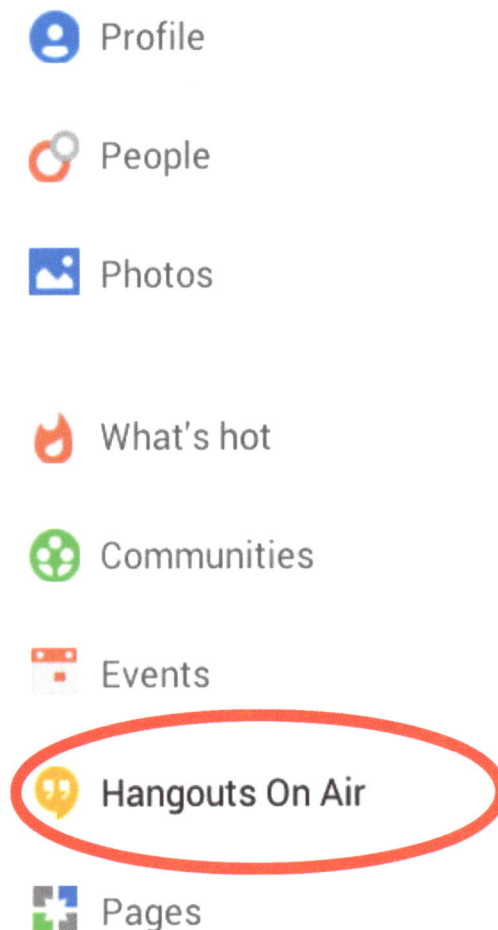

Profile

People

Photos

What's hot

Communities

Events

Hangouts On Air

Pages

Figure 6.11: Hangouts On Air

Then click Start a Hangout On Air (see Figure 6.12).

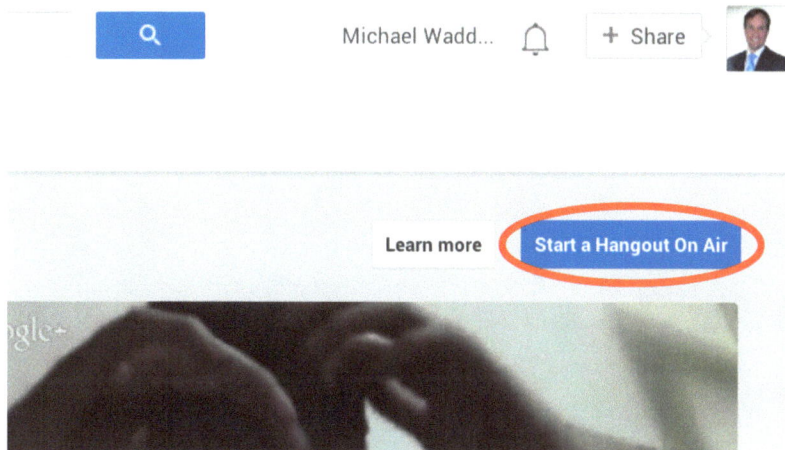

Figure 6.12: Start a Hangout On Air

Another method to host a Hangout is to set up a Google+ Event. We will show you how to create a Hangout using Events now, and will cover how to schedule Events later. First, click on "Events" on the left side menu (see Figure 6.13).

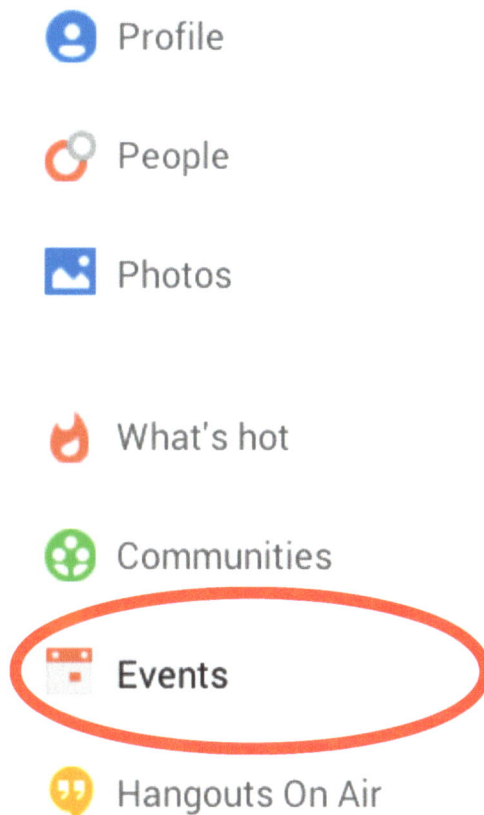

Figure 6.13: Events

Then click on "Plan a Hangout" (see Figure 6.14).

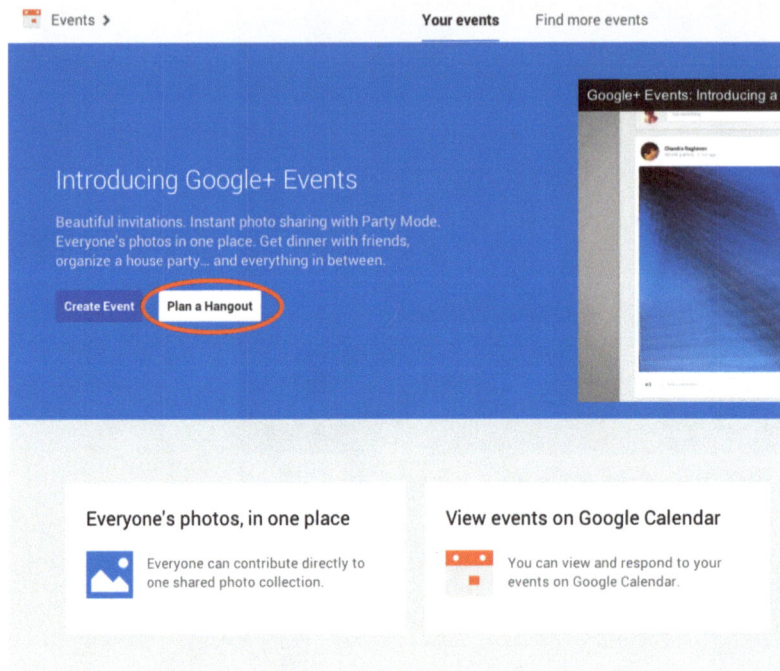

Figure 6.14: Plan a Hangout using Events

This takes you to the set-up screen (see Figure 6.15):

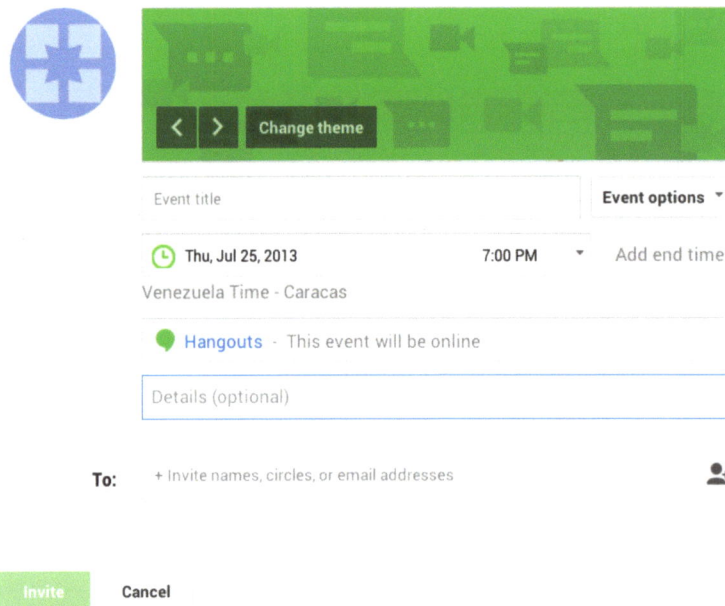

Figure 6.15: Hangout set-up screen

Fill in the details of your Hangout (see Figure 6.16).

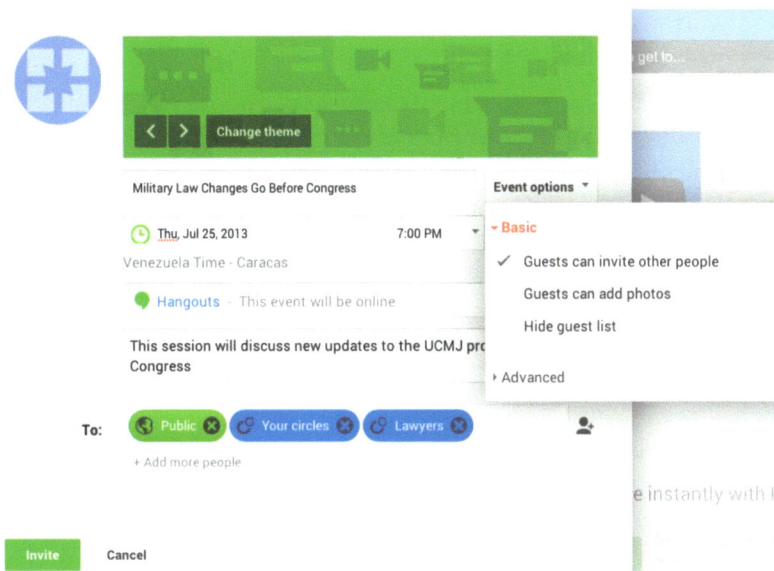

Figure 6.16: Hangout details

For this particular event, we selected the Lawyers, Public, and Your Circles as invitees. Our goal is to educate other lawyers and potential clients about current military law issues. Under the drop-down, "Event options," we selected "Guests can invite other people." The more the merrier (up to the ten person limit set by Google+) since we're raising awareness and marketing to get new clients. When you are done, click "Invite." The invitation is sent immediately.

You'll then see the following event page (see Figure 6.17):

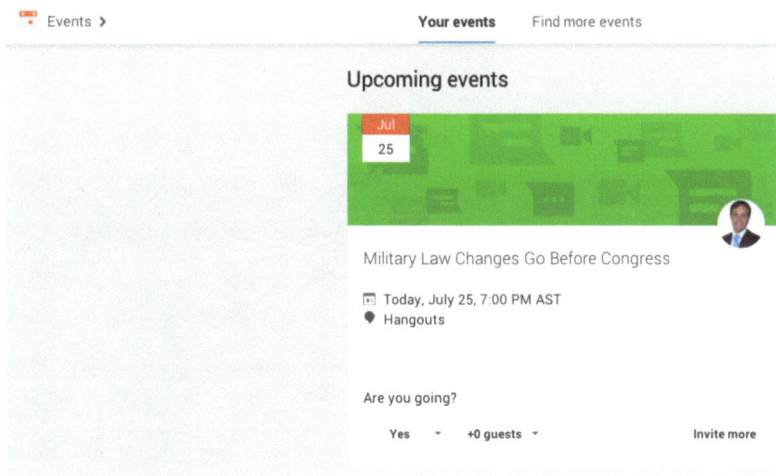

Figure 6.17: Event page

Your invitees receive a notification of the Event. When your invitees respond, you receive a notification. Open the notification to see who's coming to your Hangout. You can then visit their profile by clicking on it.

When it's time for the Hangout, click on it in "Events" and then click on "Join Hangout."

You may have to wait a moment for other attendees to join. Once they do, you will see their video image appear at the bottom of the screen.

The person speaking is shown in the larger view and the other participants are shown at the bottom in smaller view. There are several convenient options to use in Hangouts. We will explain the more useful options below.

Hangout Options: Chat, Capture, and Camera (See Figure 6.18)

1. Chat: Allows you to text chat with other participants, either all together or one-on-one.

2. Group chat: This is the window where the chats take place. The box in the lower part of the chat screen is where you type your text.

3. Capture: Allows you to take still photos of the video conference. The number in red next to the "Capture" option indicates how many captures you have taken.

4. Camera: Click on the camera icon to take a capture.

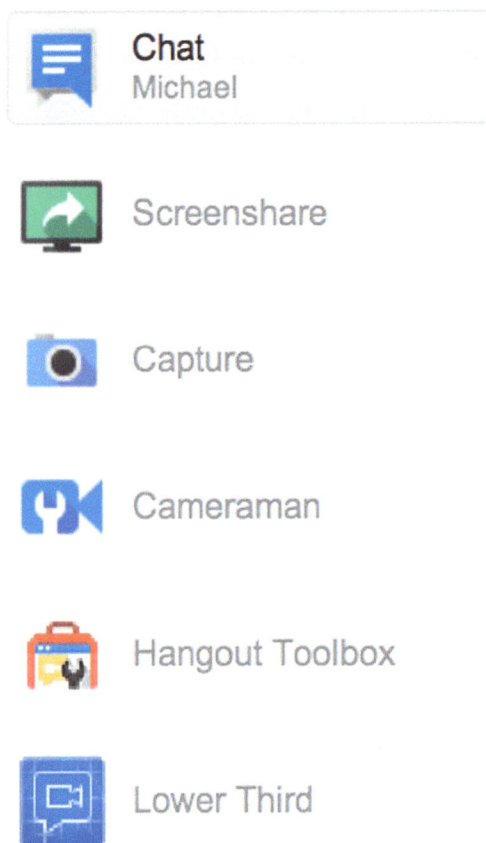

Figure 6.18: Google+ Hangout Options

Typing "/?" in the chat box brings up the menu of chat commands.

The captures are stored in an album in your photos tab. They're also sent to each participant's album. Click on "Photos" from the left-side menu and then "Albums" along the top. Then select the photo album with your captures.

The next Hangout option we will cover is "Screenshare." This is where you can share a screen, live, with your participants. It's beneficial if you have to show them parts of a document or a flow chart to help make your point.

Click on the "Screenshare" option and you get different types of sharing options from which to choose. Your options include "Full screen" or a screen of whatever files you have open at the time.

Lastly, there is an option called "Hangouts on Air." This is a public broadcast of Hangouts specifically created to be public. While there may be a small amount of value here, the possible distractions of random people popping in and out of your Hangout overshadow the value. Therefore, we're not covering it here.

Hangouts can be set up for just two people, you and a client or prospective client, for example. You can hold initial consultations or follow-ups. This is very convenient if you have clients or would-be clients who do not drive or have mobility issues. It's also pretty handy if you are just starting out and working from a home office.

GOOGLE+ TIP

Before conducting a video Hangout, you should test your microphone and lighting. In most cases, you will have to adjust the lights until you get the best outcome. For professional looking lighting, you should purchase an inexpensive light kit from Amazon.com.

GOOGLE+ TIP

When you are hosting a Hangout, make sure you are dressed professionally and have a professional background such as a bookshelf, a wall with diplomas, or a neutral colored wall. Otherwise, you may not be taken seriously. For example, lawyers should not conduct a Hangout wearing a tattered t-shirt and looking like they just got out of bed. Filming the Hangout in your bathroom or living room with children running in the background is also not a good idea. You should film Hangouts in a quiet location, free from distractions. Turn your cell phone off and make sure others know you are filming so they do not interrupt you.

Events

Consider Google+ another tool in your marketing toolbox. Just because Google+ can replace face-to-face seminars doesn't mean you should eliminate them altogether. In fact, planning your face-to-face events with Google+ makes them easier, via Events. Events can announce to your chosen Circles a real-life event at a physical location. They are created much the same way you created your Hangout. Instead of choosing "Create a Hangout" on the Event screen, choose "Create an Event." You'll see the following screen (see Figure 6.19):

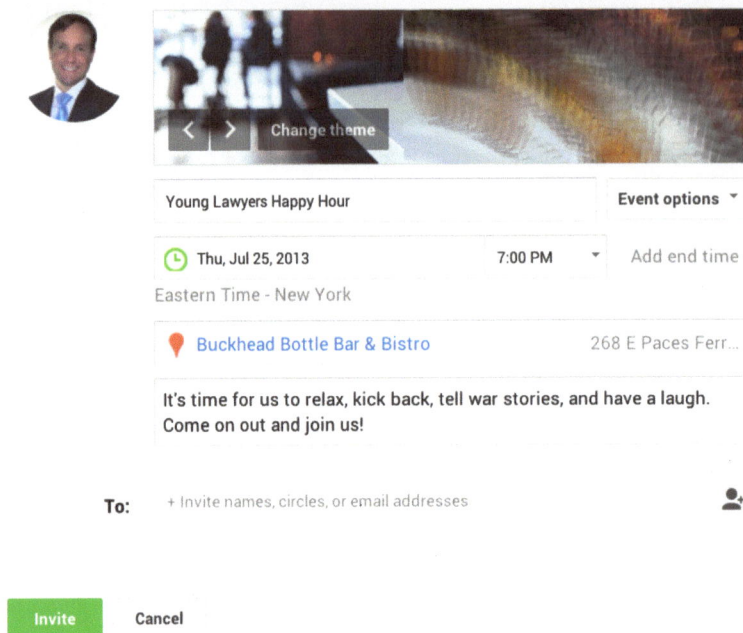

Figure 6.19: Example of Event invitation

In this example, we are obviously not inviting clients, though prospective client seminars require the same steps and information. We chose this example to show you another value of Events: Professional Networking. Not all networking takes place at Bar Association events; sometimes, it takes place at bars and other social events. This invitation works the same way the Hangout invitation did, only now you have to choose a physical location. If it's a business that's on Google, it automatically adds the address. And, it hits your invitees Google Calendars, too!

Creating Google+ Communities

You have seen the value of joining and participating in Communities on Google+. You can also create one (or more) of your own. Consider starting a Google+ Community for a general topic (mass torts), for a geographic area (Atlanta divorce lawyers), or for a unique type of practice that isn't widely represented, such as handling cases under various states' medical marijuana laws. Create a community and be surprised at how many people you reach. From the left side menu, select "Community" and click "Create community" (see Figure 6.20).

All communities   Recommended for you

Create community   🔍 Search for communities

Figure 6.20: Create a Community

This takes you to the following screen (see Figure 6.21):

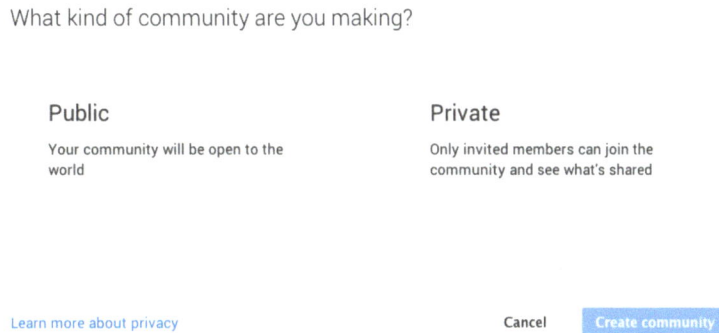

What kind of community are you making?

Public

Your community will be open to the world

Private

Only invited members can join the community and see what's shared

Learn more about privacy   Cancel   Create community

Figure 6.21: Select Public or Private Community

Google details the privacy levels for Communities on its "Create a Google+ Community" support page. https://support.google.com/plus/answer/2872671?p=community_visibility&rd=1

We suggest setting up your Community as "Private; yes, people can find it and ask to join." This makes your Community searchable to all who are looking for medical marijuana lawyers, yet you keep control of who joins. This is the best option, especially for this type of practice, to keep hijackers and spammers out, while allowing those who genuinely need your services to participate. Of course, this is a good setting for all practice areas (see Figure 6.22).

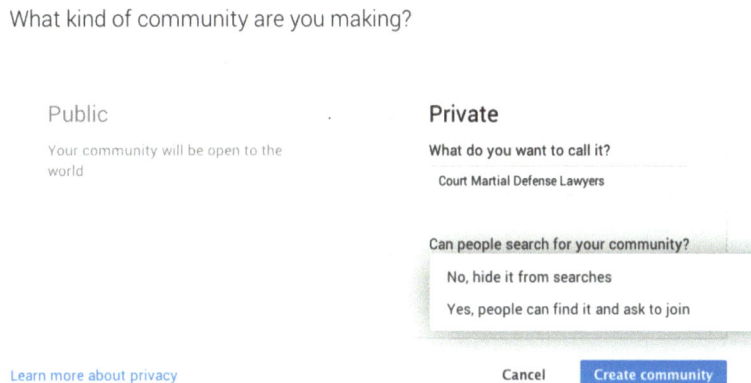

What kind of community are you making?

Public

Your community will be open to the world

Private

What do you want to call it?

Court Martial Defense Lawyers

Can people search for your community?

No, hide it from searches

Yes, people can find it and ask to join

Learn more about privacy   Cancel   Create community

Figure 6.22: Example of a private Community

When you are finished, click "Create community." If Google+ finds other, similar Communities, it asks if you want to join one of them or create your own. Click "Create your own."

The following screen appears (see Figure 6.23):

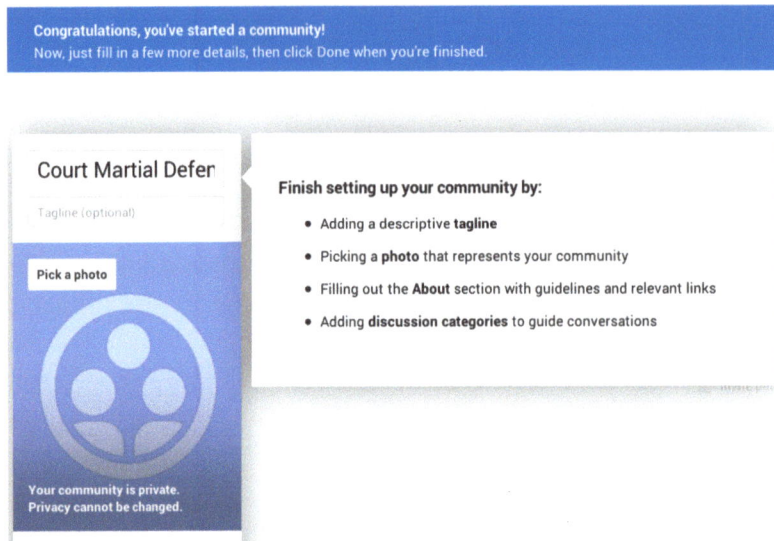

Figure 6.23: Finish setting up your Community

Add a descriptive tagline, pick a representative photo, fill out the "About" section with guidelines and relevant links (your firm's website), some discussion categories specific to your practice area, and click "Done." You now have a Community (see Figure 6.24).

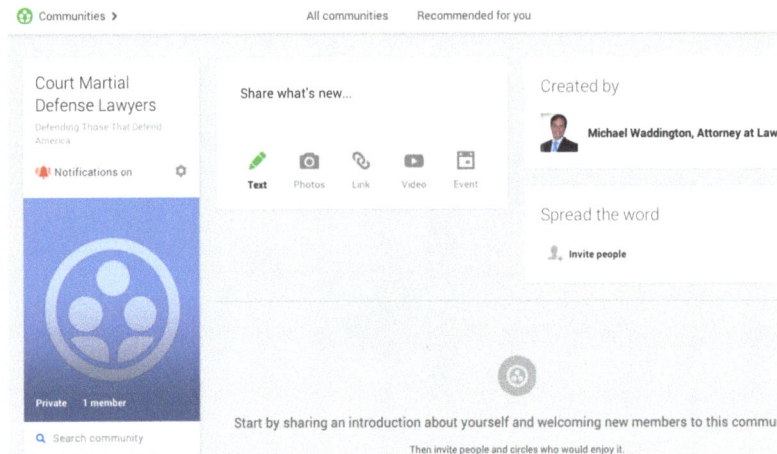

Figure 6.24: Finished Community

You invite others to join your Community by clicking on the "Invite people" button. To approve (or remove) members, click on the "Settings" button (see Figure 6.25). The screen that follows shows all members of your Community as well as those who are pending approval. Those pending approval found your Community through a search. Therefore, you have to approve them before they can participate in the Community.

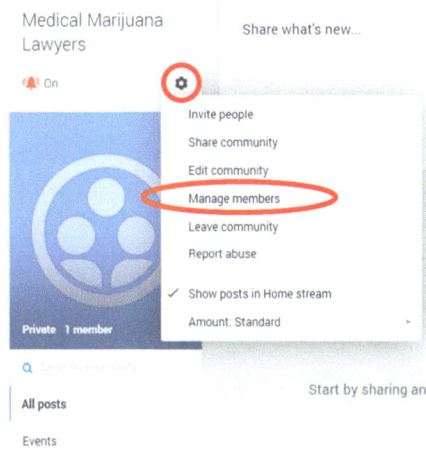

Figure 6.25: Managing members, step 1

You take action by clicking on the arrow next to a member's name. You can remove or ban members from the community. You can also promote a member to moderator.

You already know how to do everything necessary in terms of posting, etc. So go for it.

Final Thoughts

Well, there you have it. We started at "What's Google+ and what can it do for my law practice?" and ended up with you launching not only a personal profile, but a practice page, a local page and creating a Community. Keep this book handy and refer to it when necessary, no matter where you are in your marketing efforts. Additionally, there is a lot of information on Google+'s support pages that can answer your questions and help guide you along the way.

We sincerely hope you enjoyed this book. In today's competitive environment, lawyers need to leverage every opportunity to market themselves. We hope you found this book helpful.